Single?
How I found my perfect match in 90 days.

Science reveals how to tap into the spirit world and create your dream relationship.

Lisett Guevara, MSIE
Jim Gulnick, MBA

90daysoulmate.com, LLC

New Jersey, USA

Cover design by Jim Gulnick,

Cover beautification by Lisett Guevara

Photography by Amer Chaudhry
South Jersey based photographer, available for assignments worldwide.
www.amer-fotografia.net

Makeup by Shayo Olayinka
Philadelphia based makeup artistry.
www.shadesbyshayo.com

ISBN   978-0-9848000-0-1

90daysoulmate.com, LLC

Contents

Preface.... A Romance Novel (Our Story)

If you saw us today, you'd see a couple who is madly in love and happy in a thriving and supportive relationship. You may think we found each other, just like any other couple, and fell in love. That's just the tip of the iceberg. Our story is one of spiritual love but how we met is science.

I'm Jim Gulnick, and I have a master's in business administration and an undergraduate degree in electrical engineering. Lisett has a doctorate level schooling in education, a master's degree in industrial engineering, and undergraduate degree in information engineering.

We have both worked in human resources capacities, working with people and helping them through their challenges. Lisett has helped hundreds of companies, couples, and individuals in the area of interpersonal relationships utilizing her experience, doctorate education, and unique communication abilities. She has helped many friends, past students, and customers to rebuild and strengthen their marriages, open up their communication, and learn to understand themselves and each other better.

Why I described our educational background is that unlike many authors of spiritual books, we sought logical evidence that supported the seemingly magical results we personally experienced. There are certain universal laws, similar to the law of gravitation, which hold true and act in spiritual sense. Once you know how the laws work, you can use them to your advantage – to provide you the relationship you deserve.

Many of the experts in the field of personal development are simply regurgitating material of an esoteric nature. In addition, we have first hand knowledge, experience, and results from using the material that we are presenting to you. And, because of our education, engineering, and process focus, we looked for the science behind the mystery.

The end result is a Spiritual Science™, which combines belief with practical and logical steps to help you achieve what many who have used this process call miraculous results. This book helps you discover who you are, what you want, and what you want in a relationship. It helps you create your perfect match and find your soul mate.

We'd like to give you the gift of knowledge and save you years of unknowingly seeking and getting stuck in mismatched relationships.

First, let's start with our story.

Jim's Story – Mismatched.com

It was late August of 2010, and I'd been living near Dallas Fort Worth for three years but had just moved closer to the airport in May. Like a lot of single people, I had signed up for a couple of online dating sites. At first, these can be exciting and adventuresome, especially when you see several new emails. The key words there are "at first." I quickly became discouraged at the amount of time that I needed to invest. I was tired of meeting the wrong women, or perhaps I was just the wrong man. You've probably experienced the same thing: you meet a great person but nothing develops. There was always something missing.

I found profiles of interesting women and sent out winks or notes to prompt them to read my profile. We would have a few areas in common, but something would soon mismatch. And yes, I'm guilty of overlooking the differences and mismatches to focus on the similarities. Maybe you're a city person while they're an outdoor enthusiast, but hey, you both love reading. Or maybe one person loves to entertain and visit friends several times a week while the other enjoys time with couple friends or a small group. These two people both value time with others, but in different ways.

For me, time would pass and the gaps would grow in all the relationships I tried. Of course there were some really great women who were just too serious or too good for me. I also felt insecure that I had been previously married.

All this led to me becoming very selective. I no longer cared about how many women responded. I was not looking for a perpetual dating lifestyle. Who has time for that?

I added everything I could about my personality, my habits, and my interests to my profile. I included information on the type of woman I was interested in meeting. I figured I'd let the website filter out and make matches for me rather than going on a few dates to have them eventually find out the truth about me.

One day, I was looking at the pictures of those women who had seen my profile. I clicked on each one to read their profile (unlike what you may think, some men are more interested in who you are than just your looks). One profile stood out about all the others.

Her descriptions of who she was and what she was looking for were very well developed. And, they matched my likes and dislikes exceptionally well.

Coincidently, we lived only fifteen minutes away from each other. If I had not moved in May, I would have been over thirty minutes away from where she lived, and she would have not been included in my search results. Finding each other online was truly amazing. Even though I had been born in New Jersey and moved all around the US, here I was in Texas talking to a local lady who had been born in Venezuela.

We shot a few short emails back and forth and decided to meet. The rest is history. Or, should I say her story. Lisett's story.

Lisett's Story – Divorced at 27

It was 1998. I had five years in a happy, harmonious marriage. All of my friends and family called us an ideal couple, but overnight, everything was destroyed. We lacked maturity, had too much pride, and were not aware of how to work on our relationship.

As the marriage ended, I discovered that I was pregnant. I had to become a stronger woman. I needed to learn how to be more enterprising to overcome the challenges I faced from day to day. I focused on my job, my home, and my son, and drew closer with my parents and family. But, anything to do with finding a relationship was my last priority and put on hold.

Eventually I ventured into dating and spent the next thirteen years in a cycle of both good relationships and unhealthy relationships. I learned about my life, I suffered on my own, and yet I had some fun and grew from the experience. During this search process, I read books, attended training courses, and went to therapy. I met with many friends, discussed what worked and what didn't work in their relationships, and began my process of awareness. I took notes, increased my understanding of people, and developed a process to find an ideal relationship with a man who would meet me where I was, fully communicating, open and honest, and loving and caring.

Soon I became the person in my circle that friends came to for advice. They would bring their situations. I would listen, question, and provide direction. Soon, all too often, my house was filled with friends seeking advice from the person who, only a few years before, could have used a dose of the advice I was now providing.

I am sharing this story to save you from years and effort that I went through. I am hoping that you will read this book, understand the concepts, and put it to use in your life. And, in only 90 days, find your perfect match!

During my search for information and strategies for achieving success in my consulting business, I developed a broad base of knowledge that proved invaluable. I utilized methods to easily identify and achieve goals. I had written down a general description of "who I am" and "what I wanted." Occasionally I would read my notes to keep my focus. Then one day in April of 2010, I decided to apply the methods that worked so well in business to my personal life. Building from my notes, I created a specific list to find my soul mate.

I went to a hotel while I was traveling on business travel where I could relax and write without interruption. My thoughts flowed onto the paper and grew to describe the person I wanted, with each item a clue on how to find him.

Although we couldn't know it at the time, I had only begun to really focus on developing my soul mate list in April, when Jim moved Grapevine, Texas. Coincidentally, I moved to Irving, Texas and bought a house in May. Both are suburbs of Dallas, TX near the Dallas Fort Worth airport.

Finally I saved the list to my computer. When I visited a friend two months later, she suggested that I register on a dating website. At first I did not feel safe about it and discarded the idea. It took some time before I felt comfortable, and in July, I signed up filled out a profile that described me as I am, and described the person I was looking for. Soon I began receiving email from different men. Sometimes I could simply read the email and conclude this one or that one was not the man I was looking for, and other times I reviewed their profiles to make this decision.

Then I saw the photo and profile of a man whose compatibility score was over 90% according to the website! However, I didn't get up the courage to write at that moment. It was him who got the ball rolling. Two days later I received an email from this man. He was interested in my profile and would like to know more about me.

I wrote him a brief note that stated that I was a woman who loved business and I liked a good sense of humor. I asked that we could meet, and that it could be romance or strictly business, as his marketing experience in his profile was interesting to me. He suggested a meeting on Sunday at 7 am, to which I said, "He is crazy!" It was my only day off when I could sleep in, but I counter offered and we made a date on a Saturday night in a coffee shop.

When our souls first met, it was not a love at first sight. We were both cautious. Can you blame us? We knew little about each other and so we had our shields raised.

We began to talk and it was a pleasant conversation. I told him about by consulting business and he gave me some valuable marketing insights. Things were quite professional until a moment in time when I looked into his eyes. A warm feeling came over me. I felt a sense of comfort – as if we already innately knew each other – and a strong sense of connection. Do you know the feeling of being away from home for a long time and opening the door to return to a warm, comfortable spot? You walk in and immediately feel the pleasure of your home. It's safe and secure.

Wow! So it was an incredible feeling.

But, my ego told me, "Do not rush, it's just a first date." We talked about family, business, culture, country, and then it came time to say goodbye. I wanted more of this conversation. It was like I tasted a morsel of sweet cake before someone took the cake away from my plate. I couldn't wait to have a second bite.

Jim

I remember meeting at Starbucks and thinking she was not at all the type of woman I normally dated. She looked athletic and shapely and carried herself with self-assurance. We spoke about her consulting business and what obstacles she was facing as she opened her branch in

Dallas. I provided some marketing insights, a quick critique of her website, and tips for growing her business.

I was very impressed with her business. Lisett consults with manufacturing companies to help them with quality documentation, process improvement, and cost reduction. She is bilingual and travels between North and South America extensively with clients in Venezuela, Mexico, Panama and Costa Rica to name a few.

It was a really nice discussion that flowed from business to personal and back to business without any stress or direction. Then our eyes met...

Lisett

When I arrived home, I sent him a text message to say thanks, and let him know that the evening was divine. We exchanged a few pleasantries and I felt a deeper relationship was about to develop. I felt the hunger of anticipation and looked forward to meeting again.

We had our second date at Jim's house. For my part, I love cooking and I offered him a dinner at his home, with wine, candles, music and Italian food. He was quite the gentleman. Our tastes, habits and feelings were so intertwined! We were amazed at everything we had in common and how well we connected. This night was our first kiss when we said goodbye. We stood facing each other, eyes touching each other's soul, and softly kissed. His arm around my waist pulled me close. My heart leapt.

Jim

So here it was August, nearly four months since I had moved into my one bedroom apartment from my foreclosed ranch, and I had yet to unpack. Eighteen large cardboard boxes were not-so-neatly stacked against the wall. A couple of garbage bags of clothes were crumpled in the corner, with just enough pairs of pants and shirts hung in the closet to make it through the work week.

Lisett offered to come over and cook us dinner. Great! Cleaning is not one of my favorite things. (Could you tell that already?) Sometimes it gets overwhelming. But, I went from Disorganized Dan to Mr. Clean in one day, putting things away, folding clothes, and throwing out garbage just in time to have a presentable apartment for an evening dinner date.

Public humiliation has a way of getting you to do something that you wouldn't otherwise do. Try it sometime.

I had to coax Lisett into coming an hour late because I still had some finishing touches to do. I scrubbed the bathroom from ceiling to floor. New rugs and towels in matching colors warmed up the cold white ceramic.

It was worth it. The night turned out special and we had great conversation again. I walked Lisett to her car and gave her a warm hug, looked in her eyes once again, and we shared our first kiss. A soft, kind, caring, not going anywhere too fast, kind of kiss.

Time passed on. Lisett was becoming a very important part of my life, an ever changing and always refreshing break from work and living alone. We talked about everything. Nothing was off limits. Old relationships were discussed along with the good, the bad, and the ugly parts of our lives. I revealed every good and bad habit and thought I had - I figured Lisett better hear it from me now rather than have to hide something embarrassing for years to come. Extra care was taken in order to understand each other. We didn't want to miss a thing.

Lisett had to travel to South America for business. I really cared for her but at the same time I had very little fear about the relationship. Perhaps I had been so hurt before that I didn't care what happened, or maybe since we knew so much about each other that we had no worries. In either case, I was for the first time in a truly comfortable place - in love, but not feeling anxious.

Lisett

Our relationship grew more intense with every passing day. From moment to moment, our time together contained craziness, jokes, and laughter, to romance and passion. Our days were filled with a mix of a little of everything.

Too quickly, it was time for me to travel and spend about two months out of the country. My heart hurt because I didn't want to end the connection we felt.

The night before my trip, the Hispanic Chamber of Commerce was holding its national convention in Dallas. I invited Jim to attend with me. It was the first time we had been to a social function together and I did not know what to expect. I was a little nervous about so many parts of my life converging at the same time: business, travel and this romantic relationship.

We took extra time getting ready for the event. Jim played guitar and joked around as I worked on my hair and makeup. We were lost in the moment, the wonderful feelings, and ourselves. The time quickly passed and we realized we would be a bit late for the start of the program.

As we arrived at the ballroom, nearly all the tables were packed with people. Almost one thousand people, dressed in suits and attractive dresses, attended the dinner. Jim held my hand and we silently slipped into the back of the room to one of the few empty tables. The wait staff had just started serving dinner as we sat down. Perfect timing.

We enjoyed dinner, salmon with asparagus, a light lettuce leaf salad and a glass of red wine. The speakers spoke of a successful 2010 where great inroads had been made in Latino business. A famous Hispanic actress voiced her support of the organization and then turned the evening over to the salsa band.

I urged Jim to dance with me. He got up with very little prodding and surprisingly moved pretty well for a white guy, jejeje (hehehe). We moved in resonance with each other like the strings of a guitar moving in rhythm with one another. The evening became a blur of emotion. Our eyes locked together with smiles glued to our radiant faces.

This resonance and perfect sync we found while dancing captured everything we felt. There are so many times in a young relationship when something suddenly feels off. You know that moment when you have your first doubt? Jim and I didn't have those moments. Instead each passing minute felt like a step in the right direction.

The evening was winding down but our life together was just getting started. We sat back down at our table and that is when we noticed the table number... 88. We joked back and forth and then turned the number on its side. Jim said our table number was actually infinity over infinity. As the conversation continued, Jim wrote down on the back of the table number card, "Opportunity is where infinite possibilities meet infinite resources." It would truly symbolize our life and gave us the idea for our first business book. Some of the secrets contained in this simple little statement are revealed in the book you are holding in your hands right now.

"Opportunity is where infinite possibilities meet infinite resources."

It was now only eight hours before my flight, and Jim took me to a store to buy a symbolic engagement ring but we couldn't find one. We drove from store to store at two in the morning still wearing our formal attire but had no luck. So instead, we decided to buy an engagement watch to remind us that there was plenty of time for both of us.

After leaving the US, I remembered a list that I had created only a few months earlier. This was a special list I had worked on and focused on for three months. It was a list of 40 characteristics and traits that I wanted my partner to have when I was in a relationship. It was my list for finding my soul mate.

I turned on my portable computer and searched through the folders reviewing the names of thousands of files. Old consulting work projects, process documentation, and quality management information were everywhere laid out in a very orderly fashion. Although feeling proud of the business success that I enjoyed, it was the furthest from my mind. Affairs of the heart were in the forefront today.

I finally found the file entitled, "you are welcome.doc." I opened the file and slowly read each line. My eyes widened as I read the list. I was amazed. Absolutely floored. Jim possessed 40 of the 40 items I was looking for in a relationship.

The file also contained some statements of feelings that I had surrounding the relationship. They were comments, visions, or images that had popped into my head and I felt were important to note. I call these feelings and images intuition clues (i-clues™). I had written such things as "16," "161," "blue car," "white," and "butterfly."

Most surprising when I reread these items, I found that Jim and I even had more amazingly coincidental connections based on the intuition clues that I had written down! Excited, I told Jim about the list and sent it to him. What he soon discovered would change our lives.

Jim

One day Lisett told me about this list, a very specific list of 40 items that she was looking for in a man and a relationship. Her secret for developing this list, her process and methodology are contained in this book. She also used intuition to envision a few images and numbers around her perfect relationship.

These are called **intuition clues (i-clues™).** She had written down the numbers 16 and 161, a blue car, and butterfly. She did not know what any of that meant at the time she had written them down.

I think this would fascinate anyone. How was it possible that I matched all of her items, and how did the intuition clues connect to me?

Since I had matched her list of 40 items, I decided to figure out what the other items meant, assuming they had to match in some way too.

The easiest one is that I owned a blue Honda Accord. What about the numbers? I counted the number of letters in my full name and found it was exactly 16 (5+4+7). Lisett did not know my full legal name when she had told me this information. I decided to set up a spreadsheet with each letter of my name equaling a number: A=1, B=2, C=3, etc. If you add up all the letters, my name adds up to exactly 161.

Her two numbers were 16 and 161, and my name could easily create both of these exactly.

I felt the trembling of discovering something new and unique here. It was almost eerie! Now, also notice that I got the numbers on my first attempt. I didn't try a list of things that didn't work out before stumbling on to something that matched her numbers. These methods, using the number of letters in my name and adding the letters up, were the very first things I tried. I didn't go looking for something that matched the pattern after an exhaustive search. I actually found what I believe led Lisett to her vision, and came upon them immediately and with certainty.

Now for the butterfly... This was an area that could have been anything. We see butterflies everywhere. However, a few months after we met I got a job transfer to Alabama. The state mascot of Alabama is the Eastern Tiger Swallowtail butterfly...

And lastly, I typed 16, 161, blue car, butterfly into a search on the Internet and the first link that came up was a reference to a small blue butterfly found in small areas of New Jersey, my birth state.

After Lisett left on her two-month trip, I was offered a transfer to Alabama to open a new branch for my company. It was a better position with more opportunity for growth. A new eager staff filled the beautifully renovated building and they were there for me to train and lead. The cement floor had been resurfaced to shine and look like marble. The smell of fresh paint lightly filled the air.

Lisett asked me to share what I really thought because "anything was possible." Her business was just launching in Dallas, but she would consider whatever I would offer. And so I asked Lisett to join me in Alabama. She chose a relationship over her career for the first time in many years.

Lisett

This profound experience changed our lives and we decided we should write this book, share our most intimate details, and provide tools to help others find their soul mate. Everything described is a true story.

The process is real, scientifically sound, and spiritually guided. It is important to follow the steps as listed, read the material in the order presented, and complete the exercises when they appear. Each chapter prepares you for the next as the book builds upon itself giving you the knowledge required. The optimal results will be obtained by allowing the methodology and spiritual science of the book work for you.

We were married on August(8) 26(8), 2011 in Voorhees, NJ during an unforgettable week – the earth shook and heaven raved. The wedding was right between the earthquake on August 23 and the hurricane on August 28. We were blessed to have the sunlight poke through to give us a beautiful sunset in the middle of our ceremony. We are now happily married, living in a home with harmony, peace, love, health, and above all, passion. We communicate, cooperate, and celebrate every day. We hope you find yourself, your joy, your passion, and your soul mate and share your success with us soon!

"Opportunity"

(Where infinite(∞) possibilities meet infinite(∞) resources.)

Chapter 1: Why Do You Want to Find a Soul Mate?

You probably noticed Lisett was at a point in her life where she was ready to find her soul mate. She had learned and grown, studied and, maybe most importantly, she knew who she was. There are all kinds of wrong times and wrong reasons to look for a new relationship, let alone your soul mate.

Are you looking for a perfect person to come along and make you happy? Oh, I know you wouldn't say this. But reflect on it for a few minutes. On some level, don't we all want to find our soul mate to make us happy? We just have to be careful and choose to be happy before we look for our soul mate. It's not their job, it's yours! But before you start feeling down about it, let's discuss why people fall for this trap and how you can avoid it.

There is no perfect person. There is, however, a perfect person for you if you understand who you are, what you really want, and want you want in a relationship. We need to get true with ourselves and stop following the false reality set by the world around us. Then we are able to recognize our soul mate.

"There is no perfect person – there are perfect matches."

Finding your soul mate isn't about finding someone who will "fix" your life or make everything better. Someone who thinks like this might put on a fake front to attract a great person, and then let their true self out. People probably don't plan or mean to do this, but it can happen. You can

16

completely and easily avoid this by being honest with yourself about who you are (accept and love yourself!) and show this to others.

In our story, did you notice I (Jim) reached a point where I wanted my online profile to be perfectly clear and honest about who I was and who I was looking for? I filled in everything I could to give a comprehensive picture. While I was contemplating this, Lisett was meditating and creating her list. So don't worry that your potential soul mate needs to be filling out an extensive list right now. It's enough that one person is clarifying exactly what they are looking for. The other person may be creating a list, or using another way to explore who they are and who they are looking for.

I want to repeat something very important. It only takes one person to go through this process in order to find their soul mate. This process, a universal law, is so powerful that once you set it in motion your potential soul mates will start appearing. When you follow the steps in this book, it is as if you open the door to the spirit world and by your focused action reach on through to attract your soul mate to you.

Later on in the book, when you are ready, you will have the exciting opportunity to go through the same process that led us to each other. For now, let's look at why we fall into the wrong relationships so many times.

We're Set up for Failure...

For many people getting their perfect match or soul mate has become a dream. Movies portray unrealistic romantic relationships complete with intense drama, cinematographic imagery, and inspiring mood music. We sometimes create a fantasy based upon perfect two dimensional actors following a script, lit by soft seductive lighting, and in a scene finally captured on its fifteenth take and edited over eight weeks.

Books are far worse. Not limited by reality, gravity, or the laws of physics, romance novels mix intrigue, passion, and our own imagination to put us right in the middle of the story. A man who is both licensed to kill and a romantic meets a woman who is drop dead gorgeous and promiscuous. Their relationship built on the stress of the fictional situation develops within the climax of the story. The tension between them strengthens as their passion runs wild. There is no consequence for their printed relationship. We are whisked away to a delusional land where endorphins flow and temperatures rise.

One problem with all these fantasies is that the relationship simply comes out the blue without any action from the two people. They don't plan on finding a compatible relationship. They aren't seeking a relationship that is in line with their beliefs or in keeping with their personality, character, education, family, or social circle. To the contrary, they simply see each other and they're meant to be together, even if they fight it through the entire story. Why are they meant for each other, and why does this save them no matter how selfish and mean they are to each other? Is it really possible to meet the love of our life simply by bumping into them, and then have a happily-ever-ever without much effort?

We tend to judge our relationships on these misconceptions of reality. Our minds cannot tell the difference between memories created from reality or fantasy. We subconsciously compare these stories of fiction with our relationships. When the romantic tension isn't there, we don't think our relationship is real. We think the love is gone. Yet we are comparing the reality of a relationship to a fantasy and believing that the fantasy is real. We remember what it felt like to see the knight rescue the princess and when those feelings are not in our relationship – look out!

When a romantic relationship quickly turns from fantasy to reality we suddenly start finding the holes and differences, and it can fall apart. If we meet someone by chance and seem to hit it off, we might ignore the flaws or red flags at first because we're so happy to be in love.

Why are we pointing this out? Many people do not want all the drama in real life but this is exactly what they are programmed to think is how a relationship should start. A romantic story is filled with tension. We continue reading because it seems the relationship can't work out, but then it does against all odds. The grand love story evokes emotions and leaves you feeling satisfied when the couple rides off into the sunset.

A princess goes into the forest and finds a frog. She kisses the frog and it turns into a prince. She starts dating the prince and he slowly transforms back into that frog – the frog that was there all along. At first, she refused to see that he was a frog because she was in love with the idea that he really was a prince. But as they date, she can't stand his croaking and his hopping anymore. So she does what only she can do out of love. She attempts to change the frog back into the prince by offering advice everyday on how he can improve.

18

The frog prince story is an example of how many men and women go about dating. The thought of being in love, the excitement of the new relationship, and the emotions of the process keep them energized during the initial stages of dating. They are led by emotions and only after some time passes do they allow logic to enter the relationship. As they start to analyze each other they start to see there is little compatibility beneath the emotions that once were everything in the relationship.

Sometimes they work on things. They have invested time and don't want to lose everything they have. They may try to fix problems and make compromises to keep the relationship going. It would be far better to enjoy the same things, have the same goals, and work together. Without first defining who you are, what you want, and what you want in a relationship, you are subject to living a compromised life.

Imagine you order your favorite meal at a fancy restaurant (Let's hope it is not frog legs). A chef will take ingredients, prepare and combine them in a certain order, and cook the creation at a set temperature for an exact amount of time. The chef follows detailed instructions to make sure you get exactly what you want.

Through this book, we are offering you a guide to create your own unique recipe for a soul mate. You still can have that breath-taking first meeting, you still can fall in love, but now you can find the right person!

Are you committed to finding the right person for you? If we think of a relationship as a fantasy, then it will be a fantasy. It will dissolve as the light of day reveals the imperfections and problems. If we believe that our soul mate is real, then we can develop the process together to finding and creating that perfect relationship.

Tired of Being Crushed?

We are all tired of failing on the first date or afraid of starting another relationship that lasts only a week or two. Sometimes we have successfully navigated the first week or two to only reach a stalemate where we are reluctant to even attempt to build a deeper relationship. We feel that every person out there is the same and extremely superficial, and many just want to use us for money, for sex, or to fight boredom for a while until something better comes along. The fear of investing time and emotion into another relationship that may crush us is overwhelming.

Through our lives and experiences thus far, each of us may have met people who perhaps were a soul mate. Somehow or another they positively impacted us but are no longer in our lives. We must believe we learned something special from them, and now must let go of the past with fond memories. Now is the moment to focus on, our future, and find a new person, a new soul mate, to accompany us from now on.

Maybe you think finding a soul mate is just a story of fiction. But whether you want to find a partner because it is traditional, a social pressure, or just a method for non-extinction of human life forms, it still remains your dream to get that special person. You want to find a person that will share your life with you, a person that feels like part of you and can communicate with you without speaking. A person that understands how you feel without you having to explain a lot. And a person who, with a glance, connects with your entire being.

I believe that the soul mate is real. The person of your dreams is somewhere, waiting just for you. You have the chance to find that person whose soul is compatible with yours, and that person is not necessarily as hard to find as you think.

What you have done in the past might not have worked. You may have been crushed or still be afraid to fail. You might think after all these years it can't possibly happen. I am telling you, from personal experience, there is good news:

"We Have the Power to Change Our Mind Set"

We have the power to change our mindset! If we change our thoughts, we change our action, and then change our results. And in changing our mindset, we can use new tools in a logical sequence that, when followed as presented in this book, will allow you to achieve the goals that you set. If we think of a relationship as a reality, then we can create a relationship that is better than any fantasy.

The first step is to truly understand ourselves, our beliefs, values, personality, character, education, family, culture, traditions, and the society and environment in which we were raised.

The Authentic You

To discover and develop the authentic you, you need to understand who you are, what you really want, and what you want in a relationship. Soon we'll see how presenting how a false front sabotages relationships. In fact, if you want to find your soul mate but try to be someone else, you will attract someone completely wrong for you. Let's move on to Chapter 2 and take a closer look at this.

Chapter 2: Attracting What You Do Not Want

Many times you are at the mercy of the universe when you seek a person first based on their looks or one specific thing you have in common. Other times, you simply end up the victim of being set up on a blind date by someone who knows as little about you as they do the other person. You may have even chatted with someone online and feel that it is now time to go out on a date. No matter how you initially meet someone, you suffer the potential of attracting what you do not want.

"When you don't know what you want, you'll get whatever life throws at you."

Many times you may find yourself in relationships with someone who seems to be very interested in you. You smile and they smile back. You joke and laugh together. You may even find it easy to initially attract a relationship. You may have many interests and find something in common. Unfortunately, it may only be one something. Over time, your other interests may get in the way. Soon you find all the things you don't have in common and realize you again attracted what you did not want.

We must stop starting relationships until we know what we want. First we must know what is going on in our mind and understand what our heart is feeling before attempting to give our heart and soul in a new relationship. It is easy to say but more difficult to do because it is unfamiliar to us. Knowing exactly what we want means learning to read our thoughts, feelings, and true desires. This book will provide techniques on how to do the upfront work that will give you the results you want – knowing yourself so you can master your relationship rather than suffer from its haphazard ebb and flow.

We can get off track very early on, before we even begin looking for our soul mate in fact. When we feel it's time to find the perfect match for us, we go through a series of mental processes. We listen to our fears and insecurities and build a "suit" or "costume" to hide them and our true self from others. We put on a personality or begin to project what we think others are looking for, or what we think will attract the person we want (even if we don't know what we really want).

Many people play a role and dress for their part. They become human lures, trying their best to impress. They are terrified that someone may learn that they have a unique habit and so they fit into social norms as best they can. They keep their real self-hidden and will only reveal themselves if they feel safe – and if ever. Many times they are well into the relationship before they open up. Many times they find that the person they attracted by being one way is no longer attracted to their true self.

If we are to actively pursue being true to ourselves and having our outward expression be consistent with our inner self, we must begin looking inward and observe what is in our heart and mind.

Imagine that we sit on a fence between our inner world and our outer world. It is natural to face outward, observe our environment, and react to external stimulus. We are accustomed to viewing what people are saying and expressing to others around us.

Turn yourself around on that fence and look inward as you listen to these conversations. How do you feel? Why do you feel that way? What do you want to say? Begin this interior observation, look at yourself with an objective lens, and you will consciously transform your words and actions in keeping with your inner self.

The human mind automatically takes over the hunt for a new relationship, subconsciously seeking what you tell it to find. Until you fully develop what you want your mind to find, you'll be subject to the whim and fancy of your subconscious. Or perhaps, you will just attract someone who finds you attractive, passively playing no part in the search. Sometimes you find just another mismatched relationship, and these keep you from finding your soul mate.

We try to increase the chances of catching a "good prize" by dressing in our costume. The problem is people often attract the same kind of person over and over again despite changing or improving. So why do people who honestly say they want something different still end up in the same sort of relationship they just promised themselves they wouldn't ever get into again? It is because they attract people in the same way yet hope that they relationship will develop differently. If you want to change your relationships, then you must discover yourself and change who you attract.

You are unique but you are just like everyone else. Everyone has something they are afraid others will find out. When you learn to break down these barriers and become transparent before you seek a relationship, you'll find a relationship with a connection at every level.

You're thinking you don't want to date a (fill in the blank) kind of person, and yet you do.

"Why?"

We attract what our subconscious is seeking. You might feel you can only do so well. You set the bar low. After a few break ups, you expect things to be the same and even though you don't want to be in the relationship with this kind of person, it is what you know and all that you now expect.

Isn't it amazing how certain people will always attract the exact personality type they say they want to avoid? You know the person in your circle that always ends up in a relationship with a married person? Picture a fictional "Mark" who falls for women easily and seems to be chasing a different woman every few months, only to have her string him along and never commit. Then "Shelly" tends to find men with addictive personalities. Some of her boyfriends drank too much while others were workaholics or needed to go out to bars every night to watch sports.

Sometimes it's not so dramatic. Maybe you or someone you know has relationship after relationship that never developments into something deeper and lasting. That gets old after a while.

So why do people tend to attract what they're NOT looking for? It typically occurs for one of two reasons. The first is obvious. Some people are so focused on what they don't want in a relationship that they can only focus on people with those traits. The only experience they have of being in a relationship is where certain behavior is exhibited. They don't recognize people without those traits because they see no relationship potential. To them, it is not a relationship if the emotional stress and the initial feelings of attraction are not the same as in the past. Alternatives do not exist, because they don't even see those people as their "type."

The second reason people attract what they're NOT looking for is much more of a subconscious issue. They act a certain way, dress a certain way, and start relationships a certain way. For instance, say a good-looking woman wears attractive clothes, adorns herself in sparkling jewelry, and puts on her makeup like a top fashion model. She finds that only the most aggressive and self-confident men approach her. At first she is flattered but then she finds the man really only cared about her looks. Again she falls into a shallow relationship. The down-to-earth, caring, and emotionally stable man who is willing to take the time to get to know her may be intimidated by the way she presents herself. But, she keeps telling herself that next time it will be different.

A man might also attract women based on his outward appearance and social personality. His sharp clothing, high end watch, and fancy car may make him feel good about himself. He is casting a line in the water with a flashy lure. The fastest fish to bite is the one he takes home. But when the woman finds out he misrepresented himself, or when he discovers she is only interested in what his money can buy, the relationship falls apart.

While both may be successful at initiating relationships, neither one is successful in sustaining them long term. People are much deeper than their looks. The problem with dating based on outward appearance alone is that you don't know what is underneath the surface until you invest the time necessary to get to know each other. Yet, when we present ourselves as available for dating, we typically use our looks as the first tool for marketing ourselves to others. The relationship slowly develops, we become scared, and each of us hides parts of ourselves that we think the other will not like. We start feeling secure and suddenly the sparks fly when we reveal our true nature.

Self-discovery and faith in the value we offer allows us to broaden our marketing message to include our points of difference. It enables us to be upfront with the uniqueness that makes us ourselves. We go into a relationship with the truth on our sleeve and with a person that is predisposed to liking what we have to offer. What could be better?

Let's take a look at our past relationships to uncover what was good and what was not so good to help learn what attributes to keep and what to discard.

What Do You Attract?

The first step in changing something is often to identify the issue or what is going on. Take a moment to reflect on your past relationships. Make a list of each that shows what attracted you to them as well as what conflicts there were between you. You should also add a few general notes as you think about what you learned from the relationship.

Every relationship prepares us for the next. The good news is even a bad relationship can teach us something about ourselves. We learn from it and move on.

This list of past relationships isn't to be used to point out all the conflicts where you write down everything that you disliked about each person. This exercise is to help you see if you attract and are attracted to a certain personality type. We are strictly looking at elements of attraction, elements of conflict, and your reflections that will help you grow.

Your list may look something like this:

Name	Elements of attraction	Elements of conflict	My Reflection
John	Determined, fearless leader, successful, intelligent	Dominant, controlling, suspicious, jealous	As a control relationship, learning to speak directly because the communication ambiguities caused conflicts
Peter	Cheerful, fun, carefree, adventurous,	Inattention, neglected, irresponsible	Attracted to the carefree and adventurous type that were not controlling, but feeling little attention. Need to match up commitment and responsibility with fun loving personality.

Did you see any themes in your list? If so, consider if you expect this. Do you feel you need to do something different to get different results?

Now the answer is not to simply try and find different people. Now that you are beginning to understand what you attract, it's time to look within yourself.

We attract people with these characteristics because our hunting costume has a code perfect for that coupling.

In other words, we have attracted certain types of people because up until now, we have acted, dressed, talked, and walked in ways that were consistent with what was attractive to them. We may have thought we changed what we wanted but we did none of the upfront homework to change our method or modes of meeting new people.

And, it doesn't mean that you simply need to change places that you hang out, style your hair differently, pick out new clothes, meet in a new social circle, or travel far from home. Let me explain what I mean through an example, my own real life example.

Over the last ten years, I traveled throughout more than eight different countries, participated or facilitated large events, met all types of people, and attended, developed and taught a variety of courses. I joined several business associations and thoroughly enjoyed many festivals and group activities, but nothing ever happened. Lightning didn't strike. I never found a soul mate, not even a romantic relationship – **until I followed the process that is detailed in this book**.

Many of my friends questioned me, "How is it possible you know so many people and you are involved in such diverse environments, but you are still unable to find a partner?" I was asking myself the same question.

Now the questions for you are, "Do you want live in a drama filled relationship? Do you want to simply accept you're wired to attract a certain type of person? Or, would you like to choose to have a healthy relationship with harmony and balance, and where passions flow and peace exists?"

It's your choice; it's time to change your costume. It's time to break that cycle of unhealthy relationships that reduce your energy.

Getting Sucked In

A bad relationship can be a like a drug. You get addicted to the relationship and the drama, and it brings out all kinds of dark feelings and self doubt. But like a life raft, you can cling to that bad relationship, rather than float alone in an ocean of uncertainty. Sometimes it is difficult to let go of what you know and venture out on your own.

I (Lisett) clung to bad relationships even when I understood it had gone wrong. It's hard to end a relationship, though, and the process often starts the drama. That drama would change me and then I would carry it into my next relationship.

But everything is not as bad as it sounds. I learned to look at events with a more objective lens and use them as a learning experience to evolve to the next level, a level where I could identify what suit or costume I'm wearing and achieve change to attract the right person.

Another step is defining what we mean by a "perfect match." It's not a one-size-fits-all deal. You might find yourself wondering, like I did, how do I know that this is the right person? It's especially confusing if we have spent years in the search, and we have gone through many unsuccessful experiences, we become skeptical of our relationships. To add to the mess, our friends, family, and society pressure us, with "You need to establish a good relationship. When are you getting married? When will you have children? When will you start a family?"

And this is the moment when reason and emotion go head to head in an inner struggle. Reason tells you that you should not despair if you fail to establish a deep relationship with the first person you find. Logic tells you that you should be cautious after so many blows in the past. However, emotion tells you to find someone now before it's too late and you're the last single person. You have little time, you feel alone, and it seems even a bad relationship is better than no relationship at all. That is where we fall into error, because our mind is already accepting a person or relationship when it's not what you want at all. You are telling your subconscious that you "want" someone who is not right for you. Maybe they've been leading you on and it caused you to chase them even harder. You're putting on the wrong costume to find your relationship.

How do you turn things around? The power of thought and speech is amazing. We make daily decisions to co-create things. We think ideas and make them a reality. Sometimes, however, things are not exactly as we planned, and that is when the doubts begin to distort our thinking.

"Be Aware of Your Thoughts."

To begin to transform our thinking is not easy, for we must first identify what we are thinking and put ourselves into a global perspective. Develop the habit of pausing and reflecting on your thoughts. You might catch yourself in the middle of a self-defeating tirade or an energy-sucking rant about someone else. When you learn to stop and identify negative thoughts, you have the power to change them. Picture a positive outcome or think about something else entirely.

Let's say you're on your way to meet someone in person. You've passed emails back and forth, and then talked on the phone several times, and now you're meeting face to face. If you let your mind worry or prepare yourself for a bad outcome, it'll show.

You may have wanted to show up in a confident and authentic "suit," but you could not because of your deep worry. If your fear appears, then it takes over the scene. At this point you better brace yourself because the evening will probably turn out exactly as you imagined. Not so good.

Now picture the alternative. Before your meeting you start thinking positive thoughts. You may catch yourself about to entertain a negative thought and stop it. You focus on what you want.

Of course you'll find at times, attitudes and feelings that don't fall into a clear-cut positive or negative category. In this case, we need to discern if those thoughts are aligned with our true goals, and if those thoughts help show the correct suit to attract the right person.

Everything described may seem very logical and beautiful, but I imagine in your mind you're now wondering, "Uh what, how do I observe my feelings?" It is not something we typically spend much time doing. The best thing to do is to begin.

I recommend you start practicing daily to build up to at least 15 minutes of self-observation. If you're in your car for example, note your feelings generally about the day and how you feel now. Touch the texture and feel the material where the seat supports you. Listen to the sound of the radio, the sounds around you, and any noise generated by your vehicle. Breathe, smell the air, and think of what odors are present. Sense the taste in your mouth. And, watch yourself sitting in the car in relationship with the world around you.

With this exercise, your brain begins to strengthen from your practice of self-observation. You will grow your ability to perceive your six senses (feeling, touch, hearing, sight, smell, and taste). Traditionally, science talks about the five senses. But since we also have important feelings about things, we have added the sixth, and we are not talking about seeing dead people.

Once you have been practicing this training for one week, you should start applying it twice a day. Also, when you talk with someone, a friend or a family member, observe how you feel through each of the six senses.

It is important that you observe yourself objectively at the moment when you feel strong emotions. When you have dark feelings, self-doubt, and anger, or bright feelings of joy, enthusiasm, and love, you need to start watching how you incorporate these emotions into your physical posture, your body language, the words you use, and your tone of voice. Our senses are connected with our thoughts and in turn our thoughts control our communication.

All this will help you identify what you feel and discover some of your fears. The fears hide in our thoughts, protected by our egos, and need to be eradicated by self-discovery. Simply changing a word in our own mind can change how we view an event and communicate it to others.

For example, if something happens to my computer when making a presentation, I might say to a coworker, "A problem occurred with my computer when I was talking to my client. I couldn't finish showing the new products that we had in the presentation. My boss was angry and the whole thing turned into a mess. We had to set up a new meeting, but I feel like we've already lost the client."

If you change your words slightly, you might say, "I had a situation with the computer at the time I was showing my client our new products. My boss was angry, but we were able to make a new appointment. The good news is we'll now have time to better prepare the information and match it up with what we learned from the client during our meeting. I think we have a better chance to make the sale."

Simply changing "problem" to "situation" takes a load off and gives us opportunities to automatically look for positive alternatives in our brain. Instantly, we carry a lighter burden. When you change your words, you change your brain, and you change your feelings. It really is that simple.

When we have identified the right thought, we need to put it into the right words. The words must be felt and the words must be authentic. When we are connected to our words and that connection is directed by conscious thought, we have attained significant progress. Eventually our conscious direction becomes our subconscious guide.

Usually when we speak, we are emotionally spontaneous in some expressions. These moments of spontaneity can lead us to fame and glory, or it can also lead to failure. Depending on what we say and how we say it.

About that, I did not say you need to lose the spontaneity in your communication. On the contrary, spontaneous speaking is a wonderful tool if harmony, joy, and love are in control. This is where spontaneous expressions emerge helping us achieve what we want. But if there is a foundation of fear, hatred, despair, doubt, sadness, and anger, then from this fountain will flow the spontaneous expressions that hurt your soul and the people around you.

If we are to achieve conscious thought and have words that are consciously chosen, and therefore transform our expressions from within, then we must begin internal observation. We need to look at ourselves with an objective lens, a lens that allows you to see what happens every minute, every second of our mind and heart, and not invest much effort in external observation.

I remember a few years ago I had problems communicating in one of my relationships. One day I spoke to a psychologist friend. She said that I need to take notes about the topics or words that were causing the problem in our relationship. I began to watch what I said and observed my own behavior.

Sometimes when you have problems with your partner you never get tired of talking about their list of flaws, but never do you offer any self-criticism. You become the victim of that relationship and begin to distribute the blame and responsibility fully to the other. However, it is important to know that in a real relationship, responsibility for everything in the relationship is 50% - 50%. But we must accept 100% of our part of the responsibility. We must readily accept full accountability for our reactions and our input.

I started to see that it was partly my reaction, or words, that caused the problem with my partner. I understood that when I felt controlled and pressured from my partner, my thoughts were stubborn and arrogant, but in frustration I spoke with words that were not precise and created doubt in my communication. When he felt what seemed to be my insecurity, he increased his passion for creating doubt and control. The cycle continued and the drama played on.

When I watched my speech, I determined what was causing the drama and found that it was not very comfortable for the relationship. I identified some keywords like "maybe," "may," "perhaps" and changed them to more precise words such as "yes," "no," or "I cannot because..." At that moment we began clearer communication, and found increasing levels of harmony and peace. He seemed less controlling. No drama, game's over.

If we believe we have wasted time in past relationships because we didn't get married or ever live together in peace with that person, we are wrong. All of our past relationships taught us to be who we are now, and we are ready to receive our new and true relationship. You have the tools in this book, and through your action and implementation of each exercise, you can find your soul mate in only 90 days.

Attracting What You DO Want

Once you identify how you subconsciously attract relationships you don't really want, you can begin to change your thinking. As you understand more about who you are and what you want, you will start to focus on your inner self – the key to this transformation. Some people feel that if a person outwardly acts confident and beautiful others will view them that way.

This book is not about how outward appearances can attract whom you want. We are not talking about being superficial. This book helps you transform yourself internally and helps prepare your soul to find your soul mate. When a true transformation occurs, you automatically start dressing, talking, and acting in a matter consistent with the relationship that you really want to attract.

When your outer appearance is truly reflective of your inner appearance, you are ready.

The choice is yours! We told you that anything is possible. If you truly believe that, and put action behind it, you will find you can make things happen.

Chapter 3 is a reality check. You'll see how people sabotage their efforts to find a soul mate as they get started and after they meet someone.

Notes

Chapter 3: Subconscious Sabotage

The word "sabotage" pops up in novels, movies and relationships, but what does it really mean? By definition, someone who sabotages something wrecks it, all the while acting as if they are trying to help the goal. We might subconsciously sabotage things in our life because we do not really want them. They have not been internalized or they conflict with something at our core. We unknowingly take small steps to make sure the "thing" does not happen. So why do we sabotage things that we think we *do* want?

The need to be in a relationship is often distorted or disguised by our subconscious, and so starts the game and tension between what I want, what I wish, and what I have.

For example:

I would like a relationship but I also enjoy my social life as a single person.

I would like a family and to share my life with a special person, but otherwise I do not believe in those social labels of family. All that sounds complicated and full of responsibilities that I am not prepared to assume.

I would love to find my soul mate… but that means letting go of _____. (The one that got away, the one that wouldn't love me back, the one that never noticed I was in love with them.) I would have to exclude all other possible relationships and convince myself this is the one.

In order to stop your subconscious from acting against your best interest, you must be clear about what you really want and wish to make a reality. You must be ready to move forward and find your soul mate; otherwise you're working against yourself.

What happens is your subconscious doesn't want you to feel so bad. Your ever-faithful pal, the subconscious, begins to rub your back. It questions you, and plants doubt as it says in a comforting tone, "Being single is not so bad. You go to parties when you want, you have the freedom to do what you want... but if you have a relationship, can you still have a social life?"

When we determine that having a relationship is difficult, limiting and stressful, we in fact give power to our subconscious to create contradictory, frustrating and unsuccessful relationships. If we go about meeting other people with these thoughts in the back of our head, we'll become one of the people that date but hold back.

We are physically present and say we're committed, but then we start to distance ourselves at times. We keep some secrets and conveniently forget one or two special occasions because we don't want to get too close. We know it will just end up in conflict so we avoid deep connections. In essence, we want to have someone there when it's convenient. We don't want to be alone. But we don't want to move forward, share holidays, or build a foundation for our future.

If you are reading this book is not by coincidence. You are tired of those games. And, if you are aware that you want to have an authentic relationship, you have reached the first step towards your goal.

Self Examination – Are you Sabotaging?

There are many ways to sabotage yourself before you even begin your search.

Reflect on your life right now and if you have any "hang ups." Is there anything you're afraid you will lose if you enter a relationship?

If you're hanging onto something, is it possibly a crutch, an excuse so that you don't really have to look for your soul mate? Are you really afraid of looking and then failing?

Are you afraid to get hurt again?

Have you come to expect dates and relationships to fail? Maybe you're accepting the past as your future reality.

Let's take a close look at how our subconscious can sabotage our chances at finding our soul mate.

The subconscious is vigilant to react anytime, especially when you are under pressure or nervous. This is especially true when we're making a first impression with someone else. Let's say during dinner, your mind wanders and somehow you end up comparing this new person to a past partner or relationship. Maybe some little detail even triggered a memory of someone else. Without meaning to, you assume an attitude or stance. You react to this person as if you're in an old situation.

Maybe your previous partner was jealous or possessive, constantly monitoring your day-to-day activities. The new person asks, "What are your plans tomorrow?" This might just be their way of proposing a date, something fun, or only making conversation. But if you're connected with your past experiences, you might suddenly feel constricted and smothered. Your reaction is way out of proportion when compared with the innocence of the question. On some level, you may see this but the reaction happens anyway. You feel this new person also wants to control you. Even if they're simply making conversation, your subconscious believes it's still a hint that they'll soon be telling you what to do and watching your every move.

Another example is to "assume" when we meet someone. We make impressions of people every day based on their appearance or a little thing they say: A firm or soft handshake where a soft handshake signifies a "wimpy" person. But what if someone shakes your hand softly because they injured themselves the day before? Now your perception is completely wrong. Or maybe a woman in a short skirt spilled coffee on her pants, and her friend offered to let her borrow a skirt. Maybe a person in dirty or scuffed shoes helped to change a tire on the side of the road. They sacrificed their shoes in the emergency because someone needed help. We may see the person as sloppy rather than someone with a big heart who cares about helping others. It's true that we can learn about people from their appearance, but it's also true that one detail made on one day might not tell the right story.

Our subconscious uses little details to quickly paint a picture of other people. Sometimes we'll decide what the other person thinks about us within the first minute. It's a common story that two people meet for a date and do not hit it off at first. Sometimes, if they stick it out and do connect, they'll learn they were both so nervous that they sent the wrong signal.

We assume both positive and negative things about potential mates when we first meet. During the initial phase, we're trying to figure everything out and our minds fill in the blanks. We're afraid to step out of our comfort zone and ask questions. Assumptions and conjecture hinder us from communicating and asking questions.

When we meet someone, our mind is filled with assumptions and beliefs about what others think. These beliefs are false. They are not reality. They are not what the other person truly believes or thinks.

Drop Your PreTude™

The process of assuming both positive and negative things takes us to a predisposed attitude (PreTude™) that leads us to assume things and situations. A PreTude is a highly dangerous element. It is one of the main weapons of the saboteur. If the person doesn't call me, when they said they would, it makes us immediately think, "I guess that they are not interested me." In turn, we find ourselves reluctant to ask or do anything about the situation. We withdraw.

We make assumptions and speculate but we often don't take the opportunity to communicate or ask a question to clarify and uncover a deeper level of understanding. Questions, if posed with love, understanding, compassion, and tenderness generate honest answers and help both parties reach a true relationship. Imagine what might have happened if instead of withdrawing we asked with genuine concern, "Why didn't you call? Why you were late to the appointment? Or, why do you feel sad or distracted?"

Objective self-observation is the special tool we can use to combat sabotage in our new relationship. Remember that you are in a process of rebirth and re-creation; you are reprogramming your mind and your soul to receive the new person. We need to know how we really feel in order to better relate to others around us.

Finally, empathic communication that comes from within can contribute to our transformation and finally rescue us from self-sabotage. When our soul is in tune with our mind and there is inner harmony, sincere dialogue flows. When you see your own value, you see the value of the other person. If you are a very critical person towards others, then maybe you're critical towards yourself. Many times, what bothers us most about others often reflects our own internal discomfort. You should wear a compassionate lens of comprehension when speaking with others. When you value and have consideration for the other person, their importance to you will grow.

Remember, assumptions can come into play as you sit down and talk. The solution is to ask questions. These questions, if done with love, understanding, compassion and tenderness generate honest answers and help both parties reach a real relationship.

Objective self-observation is a tool we can use to combat sabotage to our new relationship. Remember that you are in a process of rebirth and re-creation; you are reprogramming your mind and your soul to receive the new person.

Empathic communication for understanding contributes to our transformation. When our soul is in tune with our mind and there is inner harmony, our empathic communication flows, considering the other person, and giving the value and importance. When you can see your own value, then you can see the value of other person.

Now, you have the opportunity to rewrite your script. You have the opportunity to strategically design your new relationship and your new experience. Only your mind, body and soul in harmony have the energy of this wonderful co-creation.

Three Steps to Defuse Sabotage
1. Don't assume, drop your PreTude
2. Use objective self-observation
3. Empathic communication

Notes

Chapter 4: Mismatched Souls

Do you remember the plot of almost any romantic comedy you've seen recently, where the protagonists seem to "miss" each other? It could be that the two main romantic leads literally keep physically missing each other such as one of them has an unexpected delay, loses the other's phone number or worse yet, gets into an accident and has amnesia. Then the other misreads the situation and anticipates the worst from the false evidence.

Or, they could figuratively keep missing each other in understanding the situation, how they truly feel about it, and the messages they send and receive. At the beginning of the story, they repeatedly miscommunicate because each is afraid to express their feelings to the other and assume the other is not interested or involved in another relationship. We feel frustrated as we know the underlying connection and laugh at the comical situations that arise out of the romantic tension that builds.

Sure, they could simply talk things out and communicate better, but the story is funny because their impressions, ideas, and assumptions keep them apart for many years. Fictional people are lucky because they have a writer who is slowly bringing them together and crafting an entertaining story.

What happens in real life when we let all these "plot devices" take over?

Mary and Tom

Tom is now 38 and single but with a "positive" attitude that says he's open to receive a new relationship. He meets a single woman about the same age named Mary, who is very friendly and cheerful.

They enter into the magical courtship phase and began going to dinner, movies and walking to the park, and the relationship grows during the first month. Both are very attracted to the other, they have relatively good communication, share many things together, and everything appears to be going very well.

Mary falls in love with Tom, his seduction process progresses to the next level. They feel on the same page, heading in the same direction. She begins to accelerate the relationship and wants to spend more time with him, share more activities with him, and get involved in the family.

But maybe they're not on the same page anymore. Tom feels things should take more time. He vaguely thinks words like rushed and pressured but doesn't share these with Mary. They just need to take a little more time getting to know each other, he decides. He begins looking for excuses to delay or cancel dates and calls her less. He starts an unconscious process of separation.

Tom feels it's too soon to say anything to Mary about slowing things down. He doesn't say anything because he fears that if he said, "Let's take things slower," she could feel hurt. It'd only cause drama. Things wouldn't slow down – she would want to spend more time together to talk it out and work through the issues to build a stronger relationship. Or maybe she would break off the relationship, and he isn't ready for that either. He just doesn't have the courage to tell her how he feels. Instead he just begins to distance himself from her while continuing the relationship.

Mary has to wonder if he's losing interest. Could it be he doesn't want to be with her at all? This fear makes her at first fight harder for the relationship. After all, if it is a good relationship, then there is no reason to waste time. Things should move forward with the two of them quickly as they are on the same path together and it must be love.

So what is going on with Tom? Why doesn't he want to move at the same pace? Why is their connection suffering? Her mind pictures him with someone else, wondering if that's the problem. Is it she's not good enough for him, or even worse, could he just be using her while two-timing? Who is he having conversations with if he is not talking about the future with her? Those thoughts make her spiteful. It's hard to show her affections while doubting him and so she pulls back and spends time picturing what he's doing, how she'll get left again and be alone. She grieves about another failed relationship and begins looking around at other possibilities since this is a dead end.

Tom, on the other hand, now feels Mary is not the same person as before. He tries to recover her connection but it's too late. She's not sure about Tom and thinks he has another relationship. Mary's distance leads him to believe she has someone else and is not interested in him anymore. Tom thinks she's no longer sincere and authentic with him as that is too much of an investment on her part in what he sadly feels to be a vanishing relationship.

Tom believes that Mary is a person of fleeting feelings who shows love one day and is cold the next. Mary thinks Tom is a closed person, cold, not wanting to take responsibility for a serious relationship. He's just another man looking for affection and sex when he's planning to leave.

Tom and Mary's speech to each other is controlled by Mr. Subconscious. Past relationships are calling the shots, and their current situation is built on assumptions. There hasn't been any deep and sincere communication. Instead, ego and pride have control and try to save them from being hurt. Tom and Mary are turned into actors playing the role that their subconscious writes for them.

Tom and Mary suffer from the PreTudes developed in their youth. Tom has very elderly parents and was born in a home with little communication. Patience was taught as the first of their values. Trust and love were built on consistent behavior over time. On the other hand, Mary's parents are a young couple who think, and speak from the attitude and programming that you should not waste time. Chances slip by, and you lose them if you do not take advantage. Mary was taught she must follow the same pattern in her life. She must take the same steps to make a home and a family, and she believes that when people lie and cheat she should be careful not to be deceived.

Maybe Tom and Mary could be a perfect match and soul mates, but subconscious sabotage won the battle and may continue to control any new relationship that Mary and Tom may have with new people.

It's easy for us to spot the issues in this story and even list some solutions. We lose this lens of clarity when it comes to our own lives, and so we require a careful reflection of ourselves. You will use the exercises that appear later on about "Who am I?" to identify values, characteristics, and programming elements that can subconsciously work against you if you aren't aware of them.

The point is that we do not jump into actively looking for matches and checking off criteria and traits of each person we meet. We in fact want to let matches come to us. The active portion of this methodology is in the self-assessment and creation of the list. Once the list is created, we then emotionally connect it to our subconscious and have faith in its attainment. The passive portion is in the fulfillment or delivery from the universe of our soul mate to us. We have to believe that once we have truly envisioned our relationship, it will be only a matter of time to when it appears.

If we let anxiety take over, then we become scared and not confident in our self. Soon our thoughts and actions are in contradiction. This contradiction is food for sabotage.

Making Matches

Okay, after all these "mismatches," you may be worried you will miss THE ONE. How do you make sure you'll recognize them? First, follow the process as documented in this book so you subconsciously and consciously visualize, believe, and feel what you are looking for in a relationship. Once you are confident and believe in yourself, in what you want, and what you want in a relationship and have created your unique list as instructed in this book, then you are ready to take action. Knowing this will allow you to observe characteristics that fit your perfect match.

You will not let looks, shape, or social standing sway you in ignoring the rest of your list. Attracting your soul mate is a much more important and deeply connected activity than dating as usual. You will be armed with a sense of pride, commitment, and uncompromising resolve in your mission. Be warned, there may be forces of nature and fate acting against you as you take control of your destiny. Don't be distracted from your goal and make sure you enjoy the way.

The first date can be very revealing, but here's another secret. Sometimes we need a second date to really see the other person. People are nervous during the first date. (Aren't you?) Both people are adjusting – maybe you've spoken online and over the phone, so you might have a mental picture that doesn't add up. That's okay. It happens. Now you have time to see this new person and get to know them. So give yourself more than one dinner or coffee meeting. You don't want to necessarily rule someone out based on a first date. At the same time, if they don't fit your list, you'll know it and want to move on quickly.

Allison ran into this situation a few years ago. She had gone through a few bad experiences and wanted to be careful this time around. She was getting to know a few different men online instead of jumping into another relationship. (This is actually smart, and a great way to look for people who match your list.) One man named Dave seemed interesting, but she didn't meet him in person for some time because she didn't feel any connection online. However, it turned out she was free one night when he asked if she'd like to go out. She agreed to meet at a popular restaurant for drinks, and possibly dinner.

When she stepped from her car, she saw Dave walking to meet her with her a wide, welcoming and handsome smile. They spent several hours discussing literature, people, and all her favorite subjects, which turned out to be his passions and hobbies too. They had dinner and went to a movie. Right from the start, they discovered they could communicate exceptionally well. She had been looking for someone who would actively listen to her and share in return. Allison might have walked away from the love of her life if she crossed him off her list in the beginning. She also remembered that she had connected really well with other men online and over the phone... but those turned into mismatched relationships. (One mysteriously disappeared for several days at a time, another had all kinds of problems so he couldn't put much into a relationship, and another was very jealous and controlling.)

Remember, some people will say what they think you want to hear rather than how they feel, so it can take time to find out if they match. Make sure you use empathic communication and listening skills to help create a more open flow of authentic dialogue from the beginning. The main objective of any good relationship is to understand and be understood.

After reflection, Allison realized she had reached a point where she knew herself well and had clarified her life goals. Through experience, she learned what kind of relationships didn't work for her. Dave was a fun individual who had also gone through some tough experiences, and he developed a philosophy that people can choose to be happy. He knew he wanted to find someone who would enjoy life with him, and not expect him to make her happy. He wanted to be successful together. Allison and Dave knew themselves, what they were looking for in a relationship, and shared frank and honest communication. They had stumbled upon a few of the relationship success secrets contained within this book.

Sometimes you might just know someone isn't right for you during the first date, but remember that we make all kinds of assumptions within a few seconds of meeting someone. Some of your assumptions might be wrong, and you could be missing your soul mate. It may be worth a second date! Get to know the person a little bit, and believe that your list will magically and subconsciously do the work for you.

The secret to this book is in not looking outwardly for your soul mate. It is:

1. Self-Observation
    a. Finding our self as we are
    b. Finding what we would like to be
    c. Defining what we want in a relationship
2. Creating a list of what we want in our soul mate
    a. Detailing the very essence that complements us
    b. Using our creative intuition to create clues
    c. Belief that our thoughts and action create reality
3. Internalizing and focus on our list
    a. Allowing our subconscious to work for us
    b. Automatic filtering external stimulus and noise
    c. Neutralizing contradictions in our observation

Sounds like you've got a lot on your plate, but it's all good! Stay on your toes, as we'll discuss more in the next chapter. Please visit 90daysoulmate.com where updates and further information are available.

I hope you are excited, because I can't wait to see what appears next!

Notes

Chapter 5: Looking in the Mirror

Have you ever stepped back from the dating scene and thought, "There has to be a better way?" Every time you meet someone new, you spend two hours getting ready, and you are nervous. You have little idea about how the date will progress and wonder if maybe, just maybe, you're on your way to meet the one. This could be it!

Sometimes a date even turns into a relationship. So what happens next? If you've dated for a while, you've no doubt run into small or large misconceptions of the other person, misrepresentations, and broken illusions. It's so easy to project qualities onto a person, sometimes because it seems to fit at first. When people meet, they'll often overlook differences or red flags, all because you really want it to work out. Other times two people meet and get along well, have a number of things in common, and begin a relationship but, sadly, it's more about having someone there rather than finding a soul mate.

What if you can save yourself from these situations by starting out right? That's what this book is about. If you begin by knowing yourself, you will know what you are looking for.

Think of yourself as a puzzle piece. There is another piece out there that fits perfectly with you. If you don't understand who you are, you might be able to define a "perfect soul mate," and even find this perfect person, but that piece may not fit with you at all! Remember, there aren't perfect people. There are perfect matches!

The Mirror of Your History

Everyone enters a relationship with a book under their arm, full of their personal history. To some extent, our history makes us who we are. How did our parents raise us? Maybe our family was one parent, a grandparent or other situation. What was our childhood like? What beliefs did we gather while growing up and then making our own life? Some of these factors can be a deal breaker in a new relationship.

Even while all these factors greatly influence us, we can always make choices about how our history affects us. Do we accept the legacy from our family? Some people say, "This is how my family did it, so this is what I want." Others say, "My family did it such and such way, and I won't ever act like that!"

There is also our adult history: our relationships, maybe a past marriage, children and how we've lived our life. All of this comes into play when we meet potential mates. Understanding your history helps you recognize if "how it was" is what you want, and why. Or maybe you want to understand why you want something different.

Although history is important and that history cannot change, we need to know it to understand, assimilate and see if we can live with it. To determine what parts of the story that you believe you cannot live without, it is important to review what you want, where we write about us. We want to have a clear pattern of what we really want so we can discern whether to continue with that person or not.

Our heart and soul goes through changes throughout our lives, they are transformed either with accidental experience or our purposeful intent, and we reflect this transformation in our actions and attitudes.

When I say that every person has a story under his arm, that each person has his book of experience, I must understand that it cannot be changed, and here the most important thing to consider is the attitude you have that person before the current relationship is starting and its history.

Discussing the history of each is an important step we must take care but there are people who say, "I do not care about your past, I do not know anything and start a new life" that may be good for a part where people do not drag past relationships to new relationships, but it is necessary to know what has happened in the past with that person, it is important to reference who are interacting and what happened in their past.

The 50/50 Energy

In the process of building the relationship you may have stumbles. There may be events that we know how to handle. Nothing happens by accident. When two people charged with energy begin to share and interact together many things can happen. The things that occur are not random. The obstacles and challenges, the opportunities and situations, result from how the two people interface with their environment based on their past story, how each is wired to react, and how their energies combine in the new relationship.

You have a unique energy about you. You emit strength, emotion, and radiate your personality and inner self to the environment. When two people get together, their energy plays together like an orchestra with each person playing notes from their own set of instruments. A harmony from their individual energies is created. The combination of the two produces a new third energy for which each is half responsible. Sometimes the energy is out of tune, falls flat in a few areas, or perfectly fits, soaring to new heights in perfect pitch with the power of a symphony.

Because our energies mix to create each situation, accept 50% responsibility for the other person's reaction in your relationship. The moment you realize that the other person acts as a mirror, or a co-creator of the event, with us in their actions and reactions, you'll gain a powerful insight and be able to demonstrate understanding of your situations and the outcomes you'll achieve.

While it is true that with a different other person their reaction might have been different, so is it true, with a different you.

How you interact with others depends on who the other is. When you are forced to speak with an ex from an old relationship, you may immediately feel a sour taste in your mouth and become cold, abrupt, and choppy with your conversation. Yet, one minute later that new prospect appears and you are warm, kind, and melodic in your tone. One saps your energy, and the other charges your batteries. You feel the difference immediately. It is as if someone flicked a light switch on and off.

The point is to stay present in your observation of your communication. Realize your role in the responsibility for creating the emotional events that ensue. And finally, understand the power you have to actively choose your reaction in any given situation.

If you look around at relationships in the beginning phases, you may notice one person is more committed than the other. Maybe one "liked" the other more and kept things going when they would have otherwise fizzled out. Sometimes the feelings are all on one side, but the other person is either too nice or to selfish to call it quits. When only one person is genuinely interested in finding a lasting relationship, it's impossible to carry on for long or to be happy in the situation.

Of course, when you're excited over a new person, it can be hard to tell if they're not so interested. They might want you to think they are for different reasons. Sometimes, deep down, you know. Something gives you a feeling. Other times you may notice some red flags such as:

- You're the one calling more often
- They'll ignore your calls but text
- They can't go on an evening date but will call late at night
- They seem hung up on someone else (in love or angry at someone)

Sometimes an honest and compassionate conversation can bring out the truth. It might get them to face the truth and you will decide together to move on. Maybe the situation isn't what you think and there have been good reasons for their behavior. Just remember, honesty above all. And equally important, take responsibility for the situation as you have played a role in its creation.

The 50% Guideline

When both people are attracted and the desires of both are aligned more than 50%, it's a good sign to move forward. You can get a feeling for this through your discussions about life and what's important to you, and if you're more serious (and looking at your list) you may even choose to write down your desires.

It's an important key to every relationship, to finding your soul mate, to find someone you can enjoy life with as you both grow. Some people will give you advice to seek someone with your same goals. This is good advice, but more than that, you want to find someone with whom you can develop goals together to achieve together. You want to find a soul mate that wants to go in the same direction, not as you, but with you.

What passes from the soul is a reflection of who we are, and that's what attracts our soul mate, when that person has looked into the mirror of our soul. When we meet that special someone, there is an element that attracts more than any other. I call it the hitch; the connection you make when the subconscious realizes this relationship can work.

Be aware of the feelings, attitudes and actions reflected from your soul. Then you can share this authentic "suit" to attract your soul mate.

When we understand that this person before us is our mirror, we know that they make us see ourselves for who we really are. It's our responsibility to grow, but our soul mate come into our lives and helps us. That's where the energy multiplies, that's where the synergy comes, and anything can happen!

Notes

Chapter 6: Time for a Change

Welcome to the process of change and creation! If you are looking for different results, do not do the same thing. If you truly desire something, but feel it's out of your reach, you won't give your all in attaining it. It is time to change! You currently have (in your very hands) the tools, the power to make the right decisions, and the power to start acting.

We cannot continue with the same attitudes and actions that we have had in the past, and one of the main elements is our belief, in who and what we think we are. If we drop a ball, does it not fall? Even if we believe with all our power that the next time we let the ball go "it will not fall," it still does. We try bigger balls and smaller balls, and yet the ball ends up in the same place – on the ground. We can't fight gravity. However, when we learn how gravity works, we can fill a balloon with helium and the balloon will float off into the heavens above.

Developing your belief therefore must be based upon science and what is possible. Your belief in yourself, your ability to change, and your commitment to your true values and skills activate the transformation process.

And, to the extent I believe in myself, in my ability to uncover a new self concept, in my power to act upon my discovery, and my power to transform myself, the more others can believe in me. This new belief about yourself is the helium in your balloon. It is what carries your soul towards the sky and attracts your soul mate to you. It works within the confines of nature's spiritual laws, aligned with the universe, and not against.

So fill yourself up with clarity, focus, and determination. You are becoming a different spirit from the inside out. When you truly know yourself others can know the real you. Take your clay and give yourself form. It's for you to choose.

Every once in a while as an exercise in self-development, my children are asked to think about what they want to be as an adult. They identify a couple of choices and we talk about these careers as a potential reality given their strengths and weaknesses. I let them do most of the talking and see what discipline they connect with the most. The goal of this exercise is to have them focus on those ideas in order to take steps towards them now.

Typically we go out and a few books on the subjects appropriate for their age level so they can explore and learn more about the subject. As they digest the information, if it fits with their core beliefs, then they assimilate it into their self-concept. They are transforming themselves closer to their goal. They picture themselves involved in the activity that interests them. They are crossing the bridge from where they are to where they want to be. New exciting information couples with existing storage areas of their brains and builds connections. New words, phrases, images, and concepts meld with old thought processes. Their brains are literally rewired and new synapses appear in response to their interests and desires.

You wouldn't say this is magic, but yet you have the same power at any stage in your life to go from where you are to where you want to be. All you have to do is take the first step – knowing where you are right now in life.

To believe in yourself, in your ability to change your values and your skills, is the activator of this process. Others can feel and sense what you believe about yourself and your power to act, your power to transform, and they will believe you when you believe you.

Friends, if you are really willing to meet your soul mate, you must believe in this process. I will give you the secrets of my experience in this book. I'm summarizing the core principles and underlying secrets of more than a thousand self-help books, courses, workshops, and training, and more than 14 years of experience and personal growth in finding my soul mate. Here you can find simple steps, techniques and the necessary ingredients to find your soul mate in 90 days.

Tuning into Ourselves...

It is easy to get caught up in the daily routine where outside stimulus and others occupy our brain space. We flip on the TV just to fill up the empty space, check the Internet for the latest news, or open email and dive into reading forwarded messages. Consider how much time you spend reading jokes and friends' status updates!

We seldom take the time to listen to ourselves think. We need to invest time in ourselves with outside input silenced. We need to stop the noise, static, and uncontrolled external messages in order to clear the way to hear our thoughts without interruption.

I know that when I drive and turn the radio off in the car at first the silence is deafening. Forced to be with myself, I start connecting with my internal voice, thoughts, and feelings. If you normally drive your car with music playing or a talk station in the background, try turning it off for a minute and see what I mean. It can be quite shocking at first as the silence opens a path to our own thoughts.

A calm, quiet connection with your mind is invaluably important when engaged in the self-development processes in this book. As we move into discovering ourselves, we need a laser-like focus on our thoughts and feelings. It's time to listen to the most helpful guide you have – you.

To do this first exercise we must be calm and relaxed, without distractions. Find some time when you are home alone. Turn off your phones, television, radio and computer. Sit in a comfortable place where you can think undisturbed. Be honest with yourself as you write down each of your thoughts, and describe each in detail with emotion.

Think about your personality, character, skills, strengths, and weaknesses. Write down your beliefs, cultural and family traditions, personal values, and habits. Be as specific as you can, as every detail is important. The chart on the following page contains some reference examples to help you in your self-observation and introspection. The main idea is to build a detailed view of yourself using the criteria that you deeply feel is most important to you.

Reference for Upcoming Exercise

AREA OF SELF-OBSERVATION	INTROSPECTION (Ideas to build upon)
FAITH AND BELIEF	Religion, involvement, daily focus, guidance
VALUES AND JUDGEMENT	Integrity, trust, respect, responsible, authority, free choice, protection
FAMILY AND CULTURAL	Importance, interaction, adherence, acceptance
SOCIAL AND COMMUNITY	Associations, groups, meetings, neighbors
FITNESS HEALTH	Exercise, shape, gym, medicine, diet
HYGIENE APPEARANCE	Fashion, hair, looks, order, habits
FINANCE AND MONEY	Saver, impulsive, investor, miser, user, giver, supporter, spender, waster
PROFESSION OCCUPATION	White collar, blue collar, student, homemaker, entrepreneur, independently wealthy, experienced
RELATIONSHIP AND BEHAVIOR	Behavior with partner, leader, co-leader, follower, couple valued
EMOTIONAL RELATIONSHIP	Strong, aggressive, mature, logical, distant, feeling, light hearted, warm
COMMUNICATION STYLE	Direct, passive, introvert, extrovert, non-confrontational, superficial, deep
ATTITUDE AND INTERACTION	Positive, proactive, negative, realist, conflicting, matching
THOUGHT PROCESS	Logical, analytical, creative, detailed, big picture, dreamer, imaginative
HOBBIES AND ACTIVITIES	Read, music, art, games, theatre, sports, clubs, technology, computer
GOALS AND CHALLENGES	Future, plans, objective, dreams, contentment
CHARACTER PERSONALITY	Image, ability, conduct, reliability, fun, serious, talkative, quiet
POLITICAL VIEWS	Liberal, moderate, conservative, independent, other

Exercise #1:

Look for a place where nobody can interrupt you and sit with pencil. You can always use your computer, but using the sheets in this book may give you a more private and personal way to detail your innermost thoughts. Plus, you'll have easy access to the chart of basic areas to help you in your analysis. And lastly, the book will help you stay away from technology and the constant connection and interruption of today's electronic world. You may find yourself taking several sessions to go through the exercises and then to build your list, and that's okay. Take your time with this exploration.

Think carefully about who you are, and begin to fill the answers to the questions below in the chart on the page that follows:

(1) Who am I?

In the first empty column, describe in detail your personality, your character, your skills, your strengths and weaknesses. Be very specific and sincere about who you really are; remember it is a document that only you are going to read.

(2) What do I really want?

In the second empty column, explain what you want in life, what your soul needs and wants to do. This is what your heart asks of you, and where your mind really wants to go. You can cover wide reaching issues about family, your professional life, social and culture items and what you will want in your relationship. Be very clear and descriptive. Write down the words as they come to you. Let your thoughts and words flow through you. This is the key to understanding what you really want in life.

AREA OF SELF-OBSERVATION	DESCRIPTION "WHO AM I"	DESCRIPTION "WHAT DO I REALLY WANT"
FAITH AND BELIEF		
VALUES AND JUDGEMENT		
FAMILY AND CULTURAL		
SOCIAL AND COMMUNITY		
FITNESS HEALTH		
HYGIENE APPEARANCE		
FINANCE AND MONEY		
PROFESSION OCCUPATION		
RELATIONSHIP AND BEHAVIOR		
EMOTIONAL RELATIONSHIP		
COMMUNICATION STYLE		
ATTITUDE AND INTERACTION		
THOUGHT PROCESS		
HOBBIES AND ACTIVITIES		
GOALS AND CHALLENGES		
CHARACTER PERSONALITY		
POLITICAL VIEWS		

Notes:

(3) What I am looking for in a relationship?

Describe the ideal relationship you desire. Begin by describing the relationship and then the person you want to be with. Think about who will complement you, and who you will be happy spending your life with. These questions and your answers will give you the foundations for the exercises to follow. Think about the details you provided in your answers to the first two questions. Build from those questions and open up to receiving the answers to your dream relationship as a complement to who you are and what you want to be.

Relationship Answers:

Exercise #2: Your "List"

Through my story, you read about how I (Lisett) developed my list. I want to share that list with you. Then, you will use your answers from Exercise #1 to create your own list.

Don't think your list needs to read like mine. I want you to see that I was specific to me, and that I wrote the list to the person I was looking for. You will want to be as honest as you can, and build your list after fully answering the questions in Exercise #1. Just as you were honest and specific in your answers, make your list as specific as possible as well.

Example: My list:

I welcome you! I'm getting ready to give you all the beautiful things and gorgeous that I have for you, much love, passion, caring, understanding.

1. Tall
2. White
3. Between 38 and 48 years (+/ - 8)
4. Light color eyes
5. Athletic body
6. Passionate for love
7. Romantic and pure of heart
8. Intelligent
9. Financially stronger or equal to me
10. Elegant
11. Good sense of humor
12. Cheerful and Happy
13. Optimistic and realistic
14. Good communication
15. Great sexual chemistry with me
16. Single or divorced
17. Faithful
18. Keeps one's word
19. Honestly, authenticity, integrity
20. Open your feeling towards me without mysteries (not afraid)
21. Colleagues and we laugh together
22. Interested in everything about me, but not jealous
23. Caring and love in his being
24. Friendly and attentive
25. Likes to dance
26. Likes music
27. Compassionate

28. Intuitive and logical balance
29. Energetic and power full body
30. Good health
31. Likes to do some exercise or sport activity
32. Has time for our relationship
33. Peace in being and wisely manages the situation
34. Spiritual and very wise
35. Be a caring teacher to learn in harmony
36. Share a prosperous and healthy life
37. Very happy and proactive
38. Have great dreams and grounded
39. Protect me emotionally
40. Educational level similar to mine

I , Lisett offer for you:

1. Much pure love
2. Felicity, happiness
3. Full of passion when in love
4. Fidelity
5. Love and understanding
6. Good communication
7. Peace, tranquility and harmony
8. Keep my body healthy and active
9. Watch for your self and detailed affection
10. Enthusiastic and positive
11. Enterprising worker
12. Spiritually elevated
13. Healing problems and conflicts
14. Elegant
15. Friendly
16. Helpful
17. Make you laugh and enjoy much
18. Home care
19. Cook delicious food for you
20. Make you more economically prosperous
21. Accompany and support you in your decisions
22. Defend as my partner to feel together
23. Be joining you in body, mind and soul
24. Respect your space and your silence
25. Share your hobbie or activities
26. Intense love
27. Do crazy things together, travel, unusual activities
28. Stick together through good and bad
29. Honor treaties
30. Keeping promises

31. Honest
32. Generous
33. Friendly
34. Not jealous but yes careful
35. Constantly renewing of the relationship.
36. Make sport together
37. Physically and spiritually integrated to you
38. Intellectual orgasms
39. Make a harmonious and loving family (your family and my family)
40. Together we help others

Clues to finding "you"

We meet in July- August 2010

Symbols: Butterflies, white or blue car, white or light blue shirt with rolled up magicians, Number 16, 161, your name contains the letter A , you like topics about technology.

Preparing to Find Your Soul Mate

Now it's your turn! Make a list of 40 items that describe your ideal soul mate and then in return your list of 40 items what you will offer to your soul mate. Use you intuition to imagine **i-clues**™ that surround your meeting with your soul mate. Put all your senses to work and emotionally connect with the infinite possibilities!

Use your answers from earlier exercise and your notes to design a list and then write it out in this book. Get ready to turn the page in your relationship story. Enjoy!

I welcome you! You are my soul mate:

1	21
2	22
3	23
4	24
5	25
6	26
7	27
8	28
9	29
10	30
11	31
12	32
13	33
14	34
15	35
16	36
17	37
18	38
19	39
20	40

And I offer you:

1	21
2	22
3	23
4	24
5	25
6	26
7	27
8	28
9	29
10	30
11	31
12	32
13	33
14	34
15	35
16	36
17	37
18	38
19	39
20	40

i-clues™:

Date Range: (for meeting)

_____

Symbols: (object, figure, color, animal, city, etc)

_____

_____

Numbers:

_____

_____

Letters: (content in name, address, etc)

_____

_____

We're not interested in actively seeking matches on what we've created. The information is to be internalized and magically work within the spirit world to change your outward aura. The list works for you from the inside out. Your belief in the science creates your reality. You've made it through the most important steps of all and listened to yourself. Congratulations and welcome to the other side of creation!

Chapter 7: Science of the Mind

Just by reading this book you've started down a path to take control of your life. You've decided you're ready to find your soul mate and have, in fact, taken the first steps to make that a reality. You may be wondering how you can completely change your life direction or affect big changes. It begins with a decision.

It's absolutely true that we are what we think. In addition to that, when we have any idea that engages our six senses and we can literally touch it, taste it, hear it, see it, smell it, and feel it deep in our soul, that thought possesses great strength and energy. That energy transforms the environment. It literally becomes reality before our eyes.

A thought or comment from another person can impact our lives and transform us. Maybe you heard a story about a friend that you thought you knew but the story changed how you felt about them forever. Or possibly you heard a speech on some subject that so moved you that you instantly changed your opinion on a matter and physically became involved in an issue or joined a group. We feel different and act differently. We take on a new identity.

In the same manner, our own thoughts impact and transform our environment and us. It can be as simple as I am tired of looking at my unkempt yard and think I should finally clean it up and have it landscaped. A magazine provides some interesting ideas, design tips, and step-by-step instructions. I purchase tools, grass seed, and plants and spend my next couple of weekends enthusiastically motivated and thoroughly engaged in my task.

Over a seemingly short period of time, the grass fills in and thickens, becoming greener. The yard takes on a clean, fresh, and flowing look. I feel good about the makeover and my neighbors compliment me. It takes a few hours a week to keep the property in top shape and I find myself looking forward to investing the time necessary to maintain my yard. I now control the yard as part of my environment. And all it took was a decision to change the look of my property.

The preceding was an obvious example on how our daily conscious choices impact our world around us. It shows how we can choose to create something beautiful from something unorganized. Like the environment around us, we can cultivate our minds in the same manner. All it takes is a decision and investment in our own development.

It's amazing how people with their energy, thoughts and words can transform an environment. When we see a group of people in a house of worship of any religion we find that some people are much more connected than others with the speaker's lessons and spirit led guidance. Those inspired people experience extraordinary feelings that stir their souls and may make them seem as one with each other and the universe. They leave worship renewed and ready to continue their day in a different state than when they arrived. This sensation of the peace that passes all understanding makes them want to return back again to regain to the lost natural state of their soul.

Some religions paint the picture that the creator is out there in the heavens acting independently from us. On the other hand, some philosophies say that the power of creation resides only within us. The truth is a lot of both.

You may have heard it said, "I am the vine, you are the branches." Imagine, that attached at your back, you are figuratively connected to each other and the universe through this vine, the unifying creator. Everything we do impacts each other and the universe as part of this universal connection.

Our ability to impact our environment and change ourselves is the power of co-creation. The term co-creation comes from the awareness that we do not act alone. The limitless creative power of the universe is able to work and flow through us when we are internally in harmony. When our mind, body, and soul act together in synchronization with the universe, we have access to unlimited resources and work as a co-creator.

Without both the vine and the branches, there are no grapes – the fruit of creation. I am here to say, we are all connected, and with the power of the universal creator flowing through us, we work to co-create reality.

Complete awareness about who we are, and what we want is the first step in this process. We must of course understand our selves, our areas of strength, and our areas of weakness (which I call "opportunities for improvement"). Then faithfully believe in continuous improvement and seek to increase our strengths and value.

"Our power to co-create is powerful."

We can improve, evolve and be better each day in a purposeful plan to establish a new vision of things, a new vision of our life. Just as we physically train our bodies and condition our legs or arms to strengthen that part, we can train our mind. If we require a specific condition for our mind, we work to achieve it with discipline, perseverance and dedication.

I remember the case of a friend, Erick, who was close to his second divorce. He told me that he was looking for answers to his situation; the reason why now his second marriage was about to end in what he considered failure. We discussed his childhood.

He was born into a home without a father figure, and his mother was uncommunicative. She didn't have the skills or knowledge to teach in a way that allowed him to understand his family condition. He was kept in the dark from what happened to his father and never discussed his feelings. He grew up under that formational framework.

All of the stimulus you experienced since and maybe even before your birth have programmed you to feel, think, and act in certain ways beyond your instinctive nature. The more traumatic, emotional, or repetitive the experience, the deeper the programming burrows. People receiving the same programs may store, associate, and react differently but nonetheless your subconscious now has its instructions.

As an adult, Erick became a teacher and began reading about programming and reprogramming of people. Inspired, he decided to establish a plan to reprogram his life to change many codes that were in his mind. Sensing the irrational behavior he was exhibiting at critical moments with his partner, he was able to identify the malicious programs one-by-one and reprogrammed his mind with new thoughts and new actions.

It was not an easy job. The first step for many of us, and for Erick, was to forgive his mother and father. Often we feel resentment, discomfort and even hatred in the subconscious for things that our parents did or did not do.

Many people, on some level, have to work through this kind of anger. Remember that your parents also had parents, and they might have gone through the same or perhaps worse situations than you. If that's the case, it might also be true that they just didn't have the right tools, experience, and history to have a great relationship with you.

When you understand that parents are also human, I hope you will find it easier to understand and, if needed, forgive them. In many cases, parents love their children but make mistakes. Your forgiveness will heal you so you can reprogram your life, your mind, and your feelings. You will then be able to view and attract that person who is waiting for your renewal.

Erick forgave his parents. Then with true and authentic love, he began to observe his actions and conduct daily practices of giving love. He knew that the best and simplest instrument was love. Without love, hate, bitterness, pride, arrogance, contempt, hostility, disgust, distrust, and fear could take root. He learned to monitor himself and activate an interior alarm whenever he began feeling these negative emotions so he could transform them back to love.

It was an arduous task that wasn't achieved in two or three days, but Erick made the marriage work. He has now been married for more than 20 years and he displays a radiance of happiness. People who knew Erick for many years say it's now a pleasure to talk to him and listen to his words of wisdom.

Erick achieved his positive transformation through reprogramming, and you can too. Just set the following four step process to memory:

1. V – Visualizing
2. B – Believing
3. F – Feeling
4. A – Action

The VBFA Process for Reprogramming

The VBFA process helps eradicate old unwanted programs and replace them with valuable self-chosen preferred programs. At first these new thought patterns are just additional paths in your brain. They become a bypass route from stimulus to a new different response – one that you choose. Over time, with Discipline, Perseverance, Passion, and Dedication (DPPD), the new thought-pathways become smoothly paved in your mind while the old patterns become overgrown with weeds to eventually recede and vanish.

Just like water running down hill, thoughts take the path of least resistance. Therefore it is important to clearly define each new path, make them wide, and faithfully practice the VBFA process.

Visualizing is one of the most useful techniques to achieving goals. Think of a soccer game without a goal. The teams would pass the ball around for 90 minutes without any reason to play. Even if all the other rules for the game still existed, they would have no knowledge of why they are playing and little motivation because they could not even attempt to score. Life has its rules whether or not we have any goals. Every day we are in the game, we might as well have a reason to play.

If you can clarify what you want, and mentally picture it, you can start working in that direction. Mentally visualizing includes what the goal looks like along with how it feels, smells, sounds, etc. Use all six of your senses in your visualization.

Great scholars and researchers have developed ideas and then transformed them into action. We can achieve the same only if we really believe in ourselves and *feel* what we believe. When we doubt ourselves, the process of visualizing begins to distort and fade so that your original idea becomes further and more distant from reality.

A visualization technique is to create writings, drawings and photographs and place them in visible places to activate your beliefs and feelings. As they say, a picture is worth a thousand words. Churches and temples have statues and pictures displayed to help members to focus their thoughts and attention. Many workplaces post motivational sayings, slogans and the company's mission to keep these fresh in employee's mind. It's even more powerful when you design and create the images and messages around you, basing them on what you want in life.

I remember over ten years ago, I created a life map for various aspects of my life. In the professional area, I wrote marks and logos of companies I wanted as clients. Now three of these companies are loyal clients with over five continuous years of working together. I also posted pictures of people at these companies who I wanted to work with and it was not by accident that I met people at those companies that were very much like the photos posted.

Believing is the next step. The power of believing in something is what allows to me to make it happen.

Before believing in something, I will believe in myself, and in my capacity of co-creation.

When I believe in my own abilities, my own strengths, my ability to improve, my ability to transform, my ability to reprogram my mind to achieve what I've visualized, then these things become reality.

To believe is closely related to feeling and acting: as I believe more in something, I start to feel and my actions are going in that direction. If I smell rain and feel a change in the air, I'll take my umbrella with me when I leave. So are true beliefs. Maybe the sky is clear and bright, but I think it's going to rain, so I go with an umbrella.

If you enjoy reading success stories of companies and celebrities, you might have noticed a common theme. So many famous people chased after their dream against the odds and so called reality. They *knew* they would make it. Many business people fail at several businesses before making one succeed on a huge level. Many actors live on hope until they get their first break.'

Feeling is like the sensations of the rain, the smell and the feel the humidity. It's the experience. So I feel what I believe. For example when I go to sleep in my bed and feel the sensation of my partner with me. It's one of the most intimate times, when we feel their body next to ours, hear them breathe and maybe snore, smell their scent and feel their warmth. Feeling an idea this way brings it into focus in a comprehensive way.

When activated, the feeling in our body begins to generate a special energy, and that energy that reflects passion, a passion for doing things, passion for each gesture or action you make. If I go to the streets with passion and excitement each day, that'll be shining my aura, my eyes, my smile. It activates a revolution of emotions. Just be careful as it may attract more than one person! You must then be capable of a wise choice.

Action! What is a thought or idea without action? If we do not act, we lose all the previous steps. This book provides you with a technique to clarify what you want and gives you tips on how to take steps and make big changes. But if you stop there, nothing really changes, does it? If you learn and grow, but keep the new you inside yourself, others will treat you as they always have.

Action includes changing your mindset and then finding ways to meet people: registering on a dating site, signing up for a sport, course, conference or club.

This is action, out on the street every day with the right costume, the new programming, vision, passion and the feeling that the connection is ready to be made. You only need to find and start your new and successful relationship.

Notes

Chapter 8: The Ghosts of our Ancestors

When my friends reveal their stories of strained relationships, I sometimes hear them talk about what I call the "ghosts of our ancestors." This is the information that was downloaded to us with the DNA that we share with our parents, fed to us through the stimulus we received in the womb, and sent to us day-by-day since the day we were born in the messages received from our parents. Messages that were deliberate or accidental, verbal or physical, and conscious or subconscious.

Many of our ghosts are activated when we meet and begin developing a relationship where we find linkage. As a relationship progresses, we find ourselves with "new" feelings, behaviors and beliefs, but these may not actually be new at all. They may be something you were programmed with early on, and they're now emerging. They were triggered when your energy and program were connected with the energy and program of the other person.

Sometimes we begin to believe that the other person has a power over us, but the reality is our program has the power over us. Our program interfaces with our partners program and may be incompatible. This is not to say that we cannot change our programs.

Jenny, who grew up in a family as the youngest of three children, didn't like to argue. She told me that she kept getting into relationships with men who always seemed to want to start arguments with her about something. We discussed her childhood to expose some of her ghosts.

It turns out that she grew up in a family with parents that argued often but were also extremely supportive of each other. They constantly told the children they were loved and the children felt even more loved after the argument ended and the tense feelings dissipated. Her parents had a deep sense of where they stood on issues and the whole family had strong personalities. Typically, the parents would sit down with the kids and discuss the dispute, the position each had, and then the resolution. Jenny grew up thinking this is how families communicated but wanted no part of the arguments.

The problem Jenny faced is that although she loved her parents and felt she grew up in a loving household, the arguments made her sick to her stomach. She associated love and openness with arguments. She thought she wanted a man with a strong personality like her parents but one who would not argue.

Time after time, Jenny would meet a man who would not argue, and she could not recreate the feeling of love that she had felt her parents possessed. After only a short time in the relationship, she would no longer feel that initial spark and she'd end it. Other times, Jenny would be attracted to a man with a strong personality that would take strong positions and she would feel deeply about him. But, after a number of months, and after a few arguments, she could no longer take the pain of the relationship. If she understood her program of attraction, she might have recognized the underlying linkage and noticed signs of conflict and tension immediately so she wouldn't mistake discord as compatibility.

Without tension in communication, Jenny thought there was no potential for a deep loving relationship. However, once she understood her ghosts, she decided to look at other areas for compatibility. She dove into self-analysis and determined dozens of other important criteria for developing a connection.

A relationship transforms us, as we get closer. The new attitudes, actions, and words create different situations that neither partner controls. It is the ghosts of our ancestors that speak through us, and the programs we run that lead us, as we lose contact with our soul.

I remember when a woman I was counseling, Elizabeth, told me that her husband had a power over her and she could not control her decisions. Elizabeth was born in a home with parents who strongly believed that marriage is until death do us part. So even if there is no compassion or love in that relationship, you must remain united.

Elizabeth lives in complete chaos with her husband Joseph. Hatred, rejection, conflict, and fighting were the norm for over 20 years. I asked her how she continued to live with someone whom she did not love. She replied with tears in her eyes, "Each time I try to detach, a force, a power bigger than me, prevents me from taking the leap."

When I told her to try to love him then, she concluded, "We know the love is over and I only feel pity for him. There is a penalty to quit and we must stay together until death do us part."

This program was recorded in her subconscious. Until Elizabeth and Joseph understand their programming and do something about it, they will not be able to be happy.

Even now, they remain the same. Elizabeth is my friend and I have offered the tools and support to help, however she has refused to change. There is an important step necessary to improve your program. You must make a real decision to change it; nobody can do it for you. It must be a conscious, heart-felt desire to change what is happening in your situation. Elizabeth does not want to make a change, so everything will remain the same.

Like Elizabeth, we have decisions to make. Do we want to continue to live in a world obscured by layers of information that were absorbed during our upbringing? Do we want to continue to subconsciously react and respond according to our parents' programming? Or, do we want a conscious rebirth into the person we want to become?

When a couple begins to build a relationship, the subconscious seeks to obtain an environment similar to the one that existed after birth. It expects a relationship to have the same qualities as early childhood, because that is the strongest information that is recorded. We each are looking for certain characteristics of our parents because that is what makes us feel at home.

When we are not aware of that, we tend to see our partner, and all of their virtues and errors, through the lens of our childhood home. And, if the subconscious home of our partner is extremely different, that's where our conflicts begin.

Decoding and Reprogramming

To decode and decipher parentally established behavior, identify points of commonality and difference for you and your partner in new relationships. I recommend making a list of the top ten positive and negative characteristics of your father and the same for your mother. If you were brought up in a single parent household or other living situation, then feel free to use the closest people to you that acted as your guardians who were role models, and impacted your life.

I recommend that if you have a partner, or when you find a future partner, that you do the same list and compare the characteristics. What you are looking for is comparing the male partner to the other's father and a female partner to the other's mother. The ideal linkage is 50% or more compatibility with good traits.

If the compatibility percentage is less than 50% between your parent and your partner, or what you want in a partner, then that needs to be addressed. If there are many significant differences in the characteristics, it is important to understand and decode that information. Differences that would trigger crisis in you and your partner need to be looked at for reprogramming or reinforcement.

You'll find a guide for this exercise at the end of this chapter.

I remember the case of Patricia, who was completely in love with your husband, Christian. They maintained a harmonious relationship until their first child was born. She felt the relationship was changing day-by-day, as she was pregnant, and even more when their child was born.

Christian was away much of the time while she was pregnant, and she came to think that not sleeping together was a part of being pregnant. But when they had their son, Christian was not the same husband as before. She was confused and hurt when she came to me and told me about what was happening.

I suggested that they fill out the parents exercise for both of them. When they completed their lists, she discovered that Christian's father left his mother when Christian was born, and as a result Christian kept hatred and bitterness within himself. His mother had told him a story of abandonment and cruelty. She said she did not more know of his real father, and the truth was a closely guarded secret by the family. Christian's mother remarried and his new stepfather became the only father that Christian ever had in his house growing up. He learned to despise his real father.

When Christian completed the parents' exercise, he decided to confront the truth about the hatred and resentment he had for his natural father and the gratitude he possessed for his adoptive father. He now understood that when he learned he was going to be a father, those were the feelings that surfaced and caused his distancing from his wife, Patricia.

I've seen many cases where programming from childhood intruded into a new relationship. In one instance, a man had a domineering and jealous mother and he would look at his partner expecting the same behavior. He would eventually create situations to evoke suspicion that created conflicts between the couple. His mother would also get involved in the drama and he would feel right at home. He'd subconsciously feel like he was in a real relationship.

If his partner came from a similar background where her mother was distrustful of men, then they made a strong connection, albeit destructive. Strangely, when a man is born to a jealous mother and later on meets a confident, calm and not at all jealous woman, he fails to find her interesting. There is no psychological magnetism for him.

Self-Honesty

Steve is a successful man in his professional area, an excellent, high-ranking, executive in a major international company and a determined entrepreneur. He has culture, he's highly intelligent, has a good son, two daughters, and three failed marriages. He's sometimes impulsive, extremely tidy, and has a social charisma that everyone likes.

He has a group of friends who always question, "If Steve is attractive, intelligent, and successful, then what happens to his relationships?" Steve wondered the same thing.

Some of you may look in the mirror and ask something similar, "I'm decent looking, smart, in okay shape for my age, and have a great job, so why do my relationships fizzle?" Sometimes, safety, success, power and leadership qualities take a hold of our personality and make us feel "perfect." This thinking leads one to believe, "Yes, I'm the perfect person for any relationship." It creates arrogance and skepticism within your ego that limit you from entering the process that I call "Self-Honesty."

Mr. Ego quickly answers and needs no reflection. He is our outward expression and invaluably interacts with the outside world. The moment of self-honesty requires genuine humility, that we shed all the old programs, old praise, old insults, and be completely honest with ourselves. Self-honesty is the time where we close the door to Mr. Ego and began a real dialogue with our inner self, where we recognize our strengths and weaknesses.

When Steve went through his self-honesty process, the first thing that surfaced was the fear of failure after so many failed relationships. But in the process of reflection, the ego would appear and say, "How can you be afraid of something you've lived through so many times?" And, it was true that he'd survived many relationships but he had never been honest with himself.

The process of Steve's reflection and decoding his program was interesting because unlike Elizabeth, he made the decision to change his life. He had to overcome the pride and ego that often got in the way of progress and block the process of awareness. When our ego takes over, and our consciousness asserts it is in the right, it knows we cannot be at fault. Our ego emphatically states that our partner is to blame and responsible for everything wrong that happened.

These are the symptoms of the presence of the ego that appear and lay claim to its own land. It is important that when you are in the process of self-reflection, that you listen to your own speech. Pay particular attention to how you respond when asked why a relationship failed. The rapid and immediate response that we give can be the key to discovering the hidden program that triggers our behavior. The first answer we state comes from the ego, as we assume no responsibility for our role in the failure. As we pause to reflect, we can also see what part we played.

You may blame a past breakup on your partner for not accepting you for who you are and wanting you to change. But after some time, you may also fault yourself from hiding your true self from them during the initial stages of the relationship. Perhaps you were self-conscious about some of your behaviors, interests and hobbies, thinking they were different. When you felt comfortable enough in the relationship to reveal your uniqueness, suddenly you became a "different person" in your partner's eyes. Trust and honesty were broken and could never be reclaimed.

I invite you to a self-honest, objective observation with compassion for the other person and compassion for yourself. When we are not compassionate with ourselves, seeking to understand and discover the causes of our actions, we cannot be compassionate with others.

Think of any time you were in a crisis situation. Your attitude can be one that seeks to solve the situation through harmony and love, thereby leaving a better atmosphere in your wake. Or, you may act as an inquisitor, harshly questioning and invoking responses of guilt and innocence, where we see the ego hard at work. Love enables us to remove our criticism of others and helps us focus on solutions that retain the relationship.

Recognize the love in every action.

When we learn to ensure that every action, at its essence, is love, is when we provide a map, directions, and instructions to the ego. The ego is not an enemy but a partner that labors for us under passive subconscious direction if not actively engaged by our conscious. Therefore, consciously reprogram the subconscious to direct the ego to act harmoniously with our mind, body, and soul.

To begin a process of being honest with yourself, read again what you wrote in "Who am I?" You might be surprised. There are always some clues to help us recognize that little hidden monster that holds us back from growing.

It's magic when we change our thinking internally. Our attitude and our environment change. The door opens for you to start living healthier relationships. You develop more harmonious connections. And, you attract your soul mate.

As long as we have noise in the way, we are not sure who we are, and we don't know what we want, then we will continue walking around the same streets, with the same people, and with the same problems. It's time to raise awareness and increase focus on more authentic and deeper relationships.

As human beings, we are complex, but within this complexity we can learn to understand our programming and establish healthy relationships with our partners.

We are a little bit of everything: we have a genetic code, family background, education, culture and beliefs that make us each different, with a personality and character.

We can identify each of our characteristics that activate different reactions in our relationships, and then change our responses. We can decode the programs of our ancestors so we can understand and transform ourselves.

Father and Mother Questionnaire

Prepare a list as shown in the example placing ten positive and/or negative characteristics of your parents in the blanks. If you want to assess this list against a past, present, or future partner, then also fill out the list for them. In any case, it is good information for you to know and review for and with any partner.

Look over your lists and see what is reflected in your relationships, and if any items caused tension or conflict with your partners.

EXAMPLE

No.	Your Father	Your Mother	Partner's Father	Partner's Mother
1	Helpful	Silent		
2	Active	Reserved		
3	Spiteful	Passive		
4	Strict	Conciliatory		
5	Orderly	Manipulator		
6	Aggressive	Liar		
7	Impulsive	Analytical		
8	Talkative	Helpful		
9	Controller	Elegant		
10	Sad	Conservative		

Note: You can fill in only your parents and analyze what codes caused crisis in your past relationships or fill in completely with your partner's information and analyze differences.

No.	Decoding (Differences that trigger crisis)	Action for Reprogram
1	Liar	Not all men are liars, I can believe in my partner
2	Impulsive	I think about things before saying them, I can hurt my partner
3	Conservative	I can open my feelings and actions to new ideas
4		
5		
6		

Exercise #3 – Father and Mother Questionnaire

No.	Your Father	Your Mother	Partner's Father	Partner's Mother
1				
2				
3				
4				
5				
6				
7				
8				
9				
10				

No.	Decoding (Differences that trigger crisis)	Action for Reprogram
1		
2		
3		
4		
5		
6		

This is a time to reflect on your answers and decide if you want to make any changes in the list you created for finding your soul mate. As time goes by, and we learn through listening to our self, feel free to change your list. We are actively involved in creation; take the driver's seat!

Notes

Chapter 9: Creationism

Creationism is a belief that thoughts can become reality. In this book we showed you how to define what you want in a relationship. When you wrote down your wants, you put in motion forces of nature. When you emotionally connected to your list of wants, and you believe that you will find your soul mate, you are programming your subconscious to automatically look for matches. You will now find yourself attracting a reality in keeping with your thoughts.

You can create your own reality from just your thoughts. First you developed something in your mind. Next you wrote it down on paper. Now, focus yourself on the details every day. Soon you will find yourself automatically taking action that supports your belief. You will see things around you that you hadn't noticed before that are in line with your objective.

Have you ever heard the expressions "word became flesh" and "spoken into existence"? These terms apply to religion as well as new age philosophies. Why? Because that is how the universe works. An inventor starts with an idea in mind and then develops reality to fit the idea. The idea first existed in their mind, they defined it in detail and wrote it down, they believed it to be true, and it was just a matter of time and focus until it became reality.

Words are powerful. Words carry equal weight with matter. Words can build. Words can destroy. Words are of the spirit. Words are of the soul. Choose your words carefully.

A child that grows up being told daily that they are smart, strong, and kind will typically grow up with those expectations for their life. They usually end up creating a reality that fits with their beliefs. You could conclude that kids from "good homes" have a higher starting point in life and do better. It's because they were given positive programming. Of course, we have all heard of the child that has been told negative things – the one that grows up and behaves badly in keeping with their programming.

There are the exceptions to every rule; children that prosper despite their negative environment and children that self-destruct even though they seem to have everything in their favor. In these situations it is usually their self-concept and internal dialogue that separate them from being molded strictly from their environmental conditioning.

Now that we are no longer children, we are in charge of our programming. You may call this a sort of positive brainwashing – one where we are in control. We can choose our new direction; focus on achieving our new reality and we'll find things start happening in line with our vision as if by magic. But it isn't magic. It is science. One could even say a **Spiritual Science™**.

In science as in life, there are two things that occur when looking for evidence:

1) Selective Evidence – Tendency to find evidence that supports your theory and subconsciously filter out evidence that doesn't support your theory.
2) Observation Limitation – Capability of only observing patterns or behavior that you first understand.

Selective Evidence

A good example of selective evidence is with people having physical symptoms originating from mental or emotional causes. These psychosomatic illnesses result from the influence of the mind over the body, especially with respect to disease. They are convinced they are sick and suddenly their bodies display the symptoms.

Like us, these patients have the power to convert thoughts into reality. They may find a disease that aligns with a single symptom and they read more about the disease. As they conduct additional research and learn more about the disease, they subconsciously create, find, and exhibit even a greater number of corresponding symptoms. Eventually they develop the framework of an illness through their assumed symptoms that is clinically identifiable. But, when the doctor tries to say that the cause is emotional, these patients seek arguments to support their truth. They filter out any other theory or information that is not aligned with their beliefs.

Our behavior strongly follows our beliefs. When we don't believe in something, our mind can't open the door to even consider or view the new idea. We may reject it immediately and label it as "impossible." Other times, we dismiss it as with a remark, "This applies to other people but my case is different." We tend to avoid any kind of idea that is not in keeping with our patterns of belief. This constant rejection of alternative thoughts blocks us from accumulating evidence to the contrary that contradicts our convictions.

Observation Limitation

What do the numbers 1, 4, 9, 16, 25, and 36 have in common? Many know that each is a square of the sequential whole numbers 1, 2, 3, 4, 5, and 6. Some do not know this and would not immediately observe the pattern. The point is you cannot observe what you first do not understand.

Here is another example:

"El punto es que usted no puede observar lo que usted primero no entiende."

To some, math, patterns, languages, and certain subjects are not understood and so, as they appear before us, we cannot observe what they mean. Our minds automatically reject or may not even see information based on our ability to comprehend it.

I coached soccer for ten-year-old players. The first thing that new soccer players do is all run to the ball at once. That is all they know. The players would be so focused on the ball that it was difficult for them to see the open areas of the field and the location of all the other players, in order to accurately predict where the ball would go next. As a coach, I needed to teach them their positions and how they should stay in certain areas of the field to better play as a team. Next, the players learned how to pass to each other and go to where the ball was going to go.

When the players first started playing, that very first practice, they could not predict where the ball would go because they did not understand the game and what to look for on the field. They couldn't observe the information that their senses provided in context with the game. As they understood the game more, and as they utilized the input from all their senses, they were able to see and feel the patterns that developed. They were now able to react as well as predict successfully.

Spiritual Science™

You may think that you believe in the methods of Spiritual Science™. Maybe you already know this information but you have not yet seen results in your life. I ask you, does self-observation of your words, deeds, and attitudes show that they are aligned with what you want and like? Can you ensure that your external behavior and actions have not contradicted your internal beliefs? Inside, are you saying to yourself, *There are not enough men or women for me, All men or all women are the same, It is better to be single, Nobody understands me,* or *No one exists that I deserve.* All these are phrases of Sabotage. These phrases build barriers in your mind and barriers in your action. Do you put on your suit to match?

When your subconscious and your conscious are aligned to accept this new Spiritual Science™, it's time to welcome you to the endless possibilities that the universe has for you. Just at that moment when your actions, mind, and body are one, the stars of heaven highlight your soul. At that time you will not be troubled to wait for your partner, you will be ready to receive and welcome your soul mate into your life with harmony, confidence, and love.

How it Works

If you don't first develop a theory, or a guess, as to how something is, then all observations are equally important or unimportant. This is why determining what you want is so vitally important in our process.

Secondly, you will only find evidence familiar to you in the first place. There will be no breakthroughs here unless you change your point of reference. This is why completing the exercises in this book and reprogramming your subconscious will enable you to recognize your soul mate.

The Spiritual Science™ works for you like magic when looking for your soul mate. The more concisely you detail what you want in your relationship, the more likely you will find a soul mate that fulfills your every want. When you thoughtfully create and write down a list, you will quickly filter out those that may have interested you before but are wrong choices. You will quickly find evidence that matches what you are looking for. Now that you understand what you want, you're capable of observing and recognizing the patterns consistent with your desires.

Infinite possibilities exist in our life. The good news is that the universe has infinite resources at our disposal. Only, the universe doesn't know what resources to supply us with until we select and define the possibility that we want. When we define what we want "consciously" and reprogram our subconscious with focus and belief, we also define a connection point between possibilities and resources. We stop looking for the resources we don't need and we focus on the resources we want – the resources that match what we want in a relationship.

For example, there are about seven billion people on the planet. These are the resources for soul mates. We don't have to look at every single person as equal potential for our soul mate. That would be crazy. Instead, we first limit the infinite possibilities by defining what we want in a relationship. In answering what we want in a relationship, we select criteria such as age range, physical characteristics, personality, geographic constraints, education, type of employment, hobbies, and more.

As we walk down the street, our focus narrows. We ignore distractions. We realize what is important to us and we filter out the mismatches. In conversation, we immediately pick up on matches and mismatches, we automatically include or exclude, and we stop wasting time in relationships slowly going nowhere. Best of all, we now have a perfectly defined filtering mechanism to use with any one of many online dating sites.

Notes

Chapter 10: Online Dating Success

Now that you have a clear understanding of who you are, what you really want, and want you are looking for in a relationship, it's time to take the next step. You can apply the advice from our book onto many dating methods – just remember to stay true to yourself and what you want.

The advice in this book applies to finding your soul mate through different ways of meeting people. You may be comfortable being introduced to potential matches through friends or family, cousins of coworkers, or meeting someone while participating in a class, sport, or hobby. But today, many individuals turn to one of the many online dating or matching sites. This chapter offers a guide to online dating.

Online dating allows you to have access to hundreds of thousands like-minded individuals that are looking for a special someone. Finding a targeted group of potential soul mates has never been easier. Online dating gives the added benefit of screening people. Before you ever talk to them, you can screen out people you know won't be a match. You can avoid reading these profiles, to some extent, by searching with your preferences. Even when you are being very specific in what you are looking for, you still will find matches. But now, those matches will be compatible, and perhaps one will be your soul mate.

Many of us are familiar with the numerous sites available for dating. I recommend the sites that allow the most filtering and matching of potential prospects for a long-term relationship. The paid sites filter and present individuals that value finding a partner highly enough that they pay to get exclusive content. It isn't that paid sites are any better than some of the free sites; in fact we met through a free site although we had also been active on paid sites.

In marketing, there are two advertising approaches that come to mind and can be applied to online dating. The shotgun approach is when you try to initially attract everyone reading your profile by spraying a lot of generalities. The reasoning goes that you're afraid of losing any one possible prospect. The rifle approach is when you take aim at your best matches by uniquely identifying them and describing the specific traits that you're seeking. The rifle approach allows you to pin point your prospective soul mates by being very selective up front. You have invested a lot of time in developing your list, now is the time to put it to use and let it do the work for you.

As you can guess, the shotgun approach will attract many people of a great variety. The rifle approach allows you to hit the bull's eye.

Remember these three words: Show, tell, be. Show others who you are through recent and many pictures. Tell others who you are by being honest and open in your descriptions and answering all the questions fully, in your voice. Be who you are when you meet people. Let the world see exactly who you are, what you want, and what you want in a relationship. Your profile should not only spell out who you are looking for, but also what you would like them to do if interested in you and the type of relationship you want.

In real life, the "show, tell, be" method means to be honest and open from the beginning with everyone you meet. Always be true to yourself, be consistent in your actions and behavior, words and tone, and appearance and grooming.

You are connected with the infinite power of creativity through your self-observation and goal setting. Opportunities arise as you channel infinite resources to your chosen possibilities.

Show

Use a variety of recent pictures – a mix of close ups, mid-range, and long shots. Show yourself in activities that matter to you. If you are a runner, then show a picture of yourself running in a recent 5K race. If you love your pet, then include a picture with your pet by your side or on your lap. If you are a huge football fan, then show a picture of yourself wearing your sports jersey.

One advantage to posting several photos is that you'll allow others to get a fuller idea of what you look like. One picture can sometimes mislead simply because of the way the camera happens to capture us in that second. I've found that most people actually look better in person than in a picture especially when their spirit and personality are congruent with their looks. When you make a connection, you'll find another beautiful soul that sees your beautiful soul.

Many people have been tempted to use older photos or to edit pictures to look better. But you are the person you are now, and you can't edit your appearance in real life. Imagine if you spend time talking to someone, and then meet them to find they look nothing like their photo. Sometimes it's not that they looked better in their picture, but you developed a mental image that's incorrect. Remember, your soul mate will accept you and love the person you are in your entirety. This is your time! You get to show who you are and what you love, which is what you have to offer that special person. Use the Self-Honesty exercises in this book to clarify who you. Be honest with yourself, and share that honesty with others.

If you're excited about yourself and want to share, others catch your enthusiasm!

Tell

You may have limited space to describe yourself. Take the time to detail what is most important about yourself and what you want. The more specific information you provide, the easier it will be for matches to self-select themselves as potential soul mates.

Look over your answers to the exercises in this book and your list to guide you. Describe your lifestyle and favorite activities that you'll want to share with your soul mate. It's important you are concise, honest and straight to the point, using a few words that contain great significance.

When you meet someone in person, questions are one of the most powerful tools for understanding. Asking what your date thinks about different subjects, or about anything that is on your mind, shows genuine interest. It flatters the other person and gets them in the mood for real conversation. Focus on what you know about them from their profile; what interests you from your criteria, or just basic starter questions. You'll find that they will return with questions for you and you'll be on your way to feeling your way through the date.

Basic starter questions:
1. What was the town like where you were born?
2. How did you get along in school with others?
3. Do you remember any of your childhood friends?
4. What was it like growing up in your household?
5. What hobbies, sports, or activities did you participate in?

Feel free to create your own list of open-ended questions to get your date talking and opening up their mind to you.

Be

It's exciting to connect with someone who might be a potential for meeting in person. As you talk online and over the phone, you have a chance to see and feel if this person matches up with your list. At the same time, they're seeing if you match up with what they're looking for; so let the real you shine through.

When you have the chance to meet someone in person, be yourself. Let them know right away who you are by expressing yourself fully. If you have any questions, ask them. If you feel out of place, don't be afraid to end the meeting quickly.

Once you know what you want, it is in your best interest and in the best interest of the person you are meeting to be up front. If the person is your soul mate, they will know how you feel. They will be on the same page. If they are not your soul mate, then they won't understand you or what you want. It is best to find out right away if you are compatible. Don't awkwardly fight through the initial communication mismatch thinking things will get better in the future.

On the other hand, if you think your first meeting was full of nervousness and that, on a whole, the person seemed to be okay, then it doesn't hurt to meet again. Without any glaring red flags and with a few good linkages in your profiles, you may show some flexibility and chalk the first date up as a decent initial learning experience. Remember your list is to be internalized, put out to the universe, and not used as a check off document on your date.

Safety and Security

Your safety should be foremost on your mind through the entire process. We're giving you advice on finding your soul mate and how to use our system with online dating, but <u>your safety is always fully your responsibility</u>! Online dating may offer certain securities you won't find if you meet someone new at an event or party, but it also poses other issues.

Trust comes from consistent behavior over time. Make sure, as you begin to correspond with potential matches, that you remain objective about anything that doesn't add up, concerns, and red flags. The number one goal is to find a soul mate that fulfills what you are looking for in a relationship. Take your time and be diligent about filtering out the wheat from the chaff – the matches from the mismatches.

Scams

If a story changes, a profile seems too good to be true, or a good looking, romantic talking, potential match claims to need some financial assistance in order to meet you, then run, don't walk, away from the situation. Block and report the profile.

Most scams start with a very simple profile. An attractive person, typically younger than you, or wealthy and older, with very limited profile information, has only been on the dating site for a few days and many times only a few hours. Often they haven't joined the site yet and use some excuse for why they contacted you without yet joining, and give some alternative email address for contact. Typically their note to you provides you with a feeling that they didn't even read your profile.

Always look for the length of time the profile has existed. Sometimes it pays to wait a few days before responding to any contact. By then, their profile may no longer exist. And, never give a personal email address. Always respond through the site.

It is important to maintain a certain exchange of information prior to any appointment. Always get the real name, age, and where they live. Plug it into the Internet using search engines and free personal data lookups. See what you can find that tells you that they are a genuine person and not a scammer. We are talking about using some common sense in being careful but not invading someone's privacy or becoming a stalker.

Talk on the phone first, and allow time for the exchange of detailed information. There is no rush. Give yourself time so you can assess the authenticity of the information. The more you know about the other person the faster you'll learn if they are real and if there is a potential connection.

If you have any strange feelings about a recent contact, then trust your instincts. There are plenty of prospects for you. You have abundant opportunity and being careful is a good thing.

Souls want to be with Souls

The good news is that souls want to be with souls. Almost any soul would be happy with any other soul. Our souls are pure love and try to find another through the physical and mental fog created by our bodies and minds.

The only thing keeping souls from recognizing each other are our minds and physical selves layered on top of our otherwise heavenly bodies. Our minds (containing programs) and our bodies (with their DNA-created structures) filter longed-for transparent soul-to-soul connections.

When we further limit that obscured connection through a mismatched relationship, our soul will soon give up finding its mate through our partner. Why?

"The soul will seek the path of least resistance to another soul."

Picture 100 people in a room, 50 men and 50 women. The souls of the men filtered by their physical self, will mostly be attracted to the physical self of women. Once there is physical attraction, and the body filter fades away, the mind filter is left. The soul of the man has to connect with the soul of the woman on a mental level through communication. The less obstructions, the clearer the path, and the more the souls connect.

The mind connection can grow over time and the path becomes clearer for the souls to meet. If either soul finds the connection difficult, then the soul will move on to a different partner to try again. Some people claim the first filter is the mind filter and the body is the less important second filter.

If we are true to ourselves, open and honest in our communication, we can stave off the hazards of any unclear connection that may impede our growth with a new partner.

Take Your Time

While our book is about how we found our soul mate in 90 days, we don't want to rush you into accepting a relationship that isn't right for you. If you feel something is off, don't settle or waste time because you don't want to be single. You'll be spending time on a mismatched relationship while your soul mate is waiting.

If you begin a relationship but it's not what you truly want, be confident and follow your soul!

Sometimes we are at the crossroads of the mind, body, and soul, and it is important to give value to these three elements. When you have hesitations between the mind and body, give your soul the opportunity to help you make the right decision. The soul always takes you to the right place with the right person.

When you feel that moment of indecision arise, radiate your soul to the universe. Decree what you really want and deserve. Observe with your mind what is happening; your patience and wisdom will make the true way understood.

You've put a lot of time into self-discovery and creating your list. Don't waste it! Use your list and keep your desires in your heart.

Enjoy The Process

When we say, "Take your time," you may think, "That doesn't sound like fun!" But it's just the opposite! Didn't you enjoy learning and discovering about yourself? Isn't it exciting to realize what you really want? Now you will be finding people who match your beliefs and picture of a relationship. You'll feel energy and cohesion when you talk.

If you find a person who is close but not quite there, it's actually a positive thing. You know the process is working and you're attracting the right kind of people. You're getting closer! Finding a "close match" will also help you clarify even more exactly what you're looking for. You might realize there is a new item on your list, or something you know you won't be able to accept.

So, enjoy both the mistakes and successes. The road is more enjoyable when you know who you are and where you are going. If we learn to savor life with humor, enthusiasm and passion, we will truly understand and observe that life is a joy.

How Will You Know?

This is an age-old question, asked around fires long ago and kitchen tables these days. How will I know he or she is the one? That's the question threaded throughout this book, which is also part of the process you can follow to know you have arrived at the right person.

You just feel it; your soul will feel the person who is your soul mate. Relax, and let yourself go. At this point in the book if you did the exercises, practiced our recommendations, and believe in yourself, then you are transformed. You should shed your worries, as you already possess the skills and abilities, and now have the confidence to know that right person for you.

"When you find your soul mate, they will recognize you!"

90daysoulmate.com

Be part of the 90daysoulmate.com community

- Share your success story for a chance to be in our next book
- Links to products and services we personally recommend
- Calendar of events coming soon to a venue near you

Join us in sharing a message of hope and love

- Affiliate program
- Master seminar coordinator
- Certified workshop facilitator and seminar leader

Non-profit organizations

- Free training programs
- Fund raising events